The Street-wise Popular F

The Street-wise Guide
to the British Economy:

The Politics Of Britain's Present And Future

Eamonn Butler

Director of the Adam Smith Institute, London

EER

Edward Everett Root, Publishers, Brighton, 2019
In association with the Adam Smith Institute

EER

Edward Everett Root, Publishers, Co. Ltd.,
30 New Road, Brighton, Sussex, BN1 1BN, England.
www.eerpublishing.com

edwardeverettroot@yahoo.co.uk

Details of our overseas agents, and also how to order our books,
are given on our website. www.eerpublishing.com

Eamonn Butler, *The Streetwise Guide To The UK Economy: The
Politics Of Britain's Present And Future*

First published in Great Britain in 2019.
© Eamonn Butler, 2019.
This edition © Edward Everett Root 2019.

The Street-wise Popular Practical Guides, no.6.

ISBN 9781911454571 paperback
ISBN 9781911454601 hardback
ISBN 9781911454618 e book

Cover designed by Adam Smith Institute.
Book production by Head & Heart Book Design.
Printed in Great Britain by TJI Limited, Padstow, Cornwall.

The Street-wise Popular Practical Guides

Edited by Karol Sikora and John Spiers

This original paperback series provides *practical*, expert, insider-knowledge.

Each book tells you what professionals know, but which is not often shared with the public at large.

The books provide vital insider guidance, including what some authorities would prefer you never to know.

The series empowers the individual.

The authors are all internationally acknowledged professional experts and skilled popular writers.

We will be pleased to receive suggestions for other titles.

AVAILABLE.

Georgina Burnett, *The Street-wise Guide to Buying, Improving, and Selling Your Home.*

Robert Lefever, *The Street-wise Guide to Coping with and Recovering from Addiction.*

Karol Sikora, *The Street-wise Patient's Guide To Surviving Cancer. How to be an active, organised, informed, and welcomed patient.*

Gill Steel, *The Street-wise Guide to Getting the Best From Your Lawyer.*

Lady Teviot, *The Street-wise Guide to Doing Your Family History.*

FORTHCOMING.

Tom Balchin, *The Street-wise Guide to Surviving a Stroke.*

Sam Collins, *The Street-wise Guide to Choosing a Care Home.*

Stephen Davies, *The Street-wise Guide to the Devil and His Works*

Raj Persaud and Peter Bruggen, *The Street-wise Guide to Getting the Best Mental Health Care. How to Survive the Mental Health System and Get Some Proper Help.*

Nung Rudarakanchana, *The Street-wise Woman's Guide to Getting The Best Healthcare.*

About the author

Eamonn Butler is Director of the Adam Smith Institute, one of the world's leading policy think tanks. He holds degrees in economics and psychology, a PhD in philosophy, and an honorary DLitt. In the 1970s he worked for the US House of Representatives, and taught philosophy at Hillsdale College, Michigan, before returning to the UK to help found the Adam Smith Institute. A former winner of the Freedom Medal of Freedom's Foundation at Valley Forge and the UK National Free Enterprise Award, he is currently Secretary of the Mont Pelerin Society.

Eamonn is the author of many books, including introductions on the pioneering economists Adam Smith, Milton Friedman, F. A. Hayek and Ludwig von Mises. He has recently published *An Introduction to Capitalism*, and *Ayn Rand, An Introduction*. He has also published primers on Classical Liberalism, Public Choice, Magna Carta, the Austrian School of Economics and great liberal thinkers, as well as *The Condensed Wealth of Nations* and *The Best Book on the Market*. His *Foundations of a Free Society* won the 2014 Fisher Prize. His popular books include *Forty Centuries of Wage and Price Controls*, *The Rotten State of Britain*, *The Alternative Manifesto*, *The Economics of Success*, and a series of books on IQ. He is a frequent contributor to print, broadcast and online media.

Contents

ESCAPING A BAD NEIGHBOURHOOD

10. A brighter future

11. Making public policy rational

12. Ending the need to be streetwise

1 Why you need to be streetwise

What does it mean to be streetwise? It means being able to navigate your way through a hostile, threatening and dangerous neighbourhood. It means having the experience and understanding to know how things operate. It means to be aware that things are not always what they seem, and that if something looks too good to be true, it probably is. It means looking behind what people say that they are doing and working out their real motives, and the real effects of what they do. Realising that there are plenty of people posing as your friend and saviour who are really interested only in themselves and their own friends; and even if people do try to help you, they can very easily just mess you up. Being alert and savvy enough to avoid the traps that are set for the unwary. Having the know-how, agility and nous to turn the workings of a hostile neighbourhood to your own advantage.

A bad political and economic neighbourhood

Never has it been more important to be streetwise, particularly when it comes to the political and economic environment. You need to keep your wits about you. In the UK today—as in many other countries—politics and economics has become a hostile neighbourhood, an urban jungle. Political and religious fanatics trade threats of violence over Twitter, plant nail bombs on trains or run down innocent citizens on streets and bridges. Politicians take more delight in bad-mouthing their opponents or causing them embarrassment than they do in achieving anything positive for the public. The TV and radio news is dominated, not by world events, but by the street warfare between political gangs while a scornful public looks on in amazement.

The economic neighbourhood is equally scary. Like street gangs enjoying their criminal takings, the Westminster gangs spend our money like sailors. In fact, they spend even more than what they can actually squeeze out of us—and then borrow to make up the difference. Though our mothers warn us of the dangers of debt, our politicians seem to have learnt no such lesson. Not only is the UK government deep in debt, but it adds more to that debt every hour of every day. Back in 2005, the UK government owed an amount equal to roughly a third of what the nation earned in a year – 34% of Gross National Product (GDP). Most prudent economists figured that this was more than enough. Today the government owes two and a half times that figure – the equivalent of over four-fifths of GDP. In terms of hard cash, at the time of the Spring 2019 Budget, the UK government owed £1.84 trillion. Let me spell that out: £1,830,000,000. That is nearly £30,000 for every adult, child and infant, £120,000 for a family of four.

Could it be worse? It already is. That £1.84 trillion is just the debt that the government admits to. It does not count its vast and continuing commitments to pay generous (often index-linked) pensions to MPs, civil servants, local government officers, the army, the police, fire fighters, health service workers, school teachers, college lecturers and all the rest – a liability of well over a £1 trillion on its own. Then there is the ongoing cost of decommissioning old nuclear power stations. Nor does the official figure include the bank bailouts and bank liabilities still on the government's books. Network Rail's debt notches up a few more tens of billions. The future amounts that the government is contracted to pay infrastructure companies for the continuing upkeep and use of the schools, hospitals, roads and prisons constructed under the Private Finance Initiative must be reckoned in hundreds of billions. Then there are the really scary commitments that the Treasury can hardly renege on: future state pension payments, our future healthcare services, our kids' schooling and all those welfare promises to look after us if we become unemployed or get injured. Add all those in and you are talking about a national debt six or eight times the official £30,000 figure.

On top of all that, the Labour leader Jeremy Corbyn says that if he gets into power, he will spend another £500bn on infrastructure projects, borrowing the money if necessary. This is really scary.

But not only does the government have an enormous unpaid balance on the credit card. It continues to add to the total every year – the so-called 'deficit' (which is polite jargon for overspending). Indeed, its shortfall on the year to March 2019 amounted to over £20 billion. While the authorities say that such a 'modest' deficit of below 2% of GDP is 'affordable', that £20 billion is still equivalent to around £33 for every adult, child and infant in the country. Sure, UK economic growth and prosperity is still expanding, despite all the Brexit turmoil (and the economy has certainly not been the disaster that the Bank of England and the then Chancellor George Osborne warned of). So maybe the rise in our debt is affordable: but it is still unwise to keep piling on debt until it becomes unaffordable. Ordinary citizens have to pay off these debts, or pay the interest on them, through their taxes. Starting the year tens of thousands in debt and finishing it another £33 a head even deeper in debt is not something that families and taxpayers are likely to welcome. Yet the academic economists, Treasury ministers and officials, central bankers and grandees from international quangos like the International Monetary fund say things are all under control and not to worry, because they know how to engineer economic growth and rising prosperity. The general public are more sceptical. They do not think that the politicians and economists have the foggiest idea what they are doing. No wonder they are causing trouble for them at the polls.

In continental Europe, meanwhile, the Euro zone has been lurching from crisis to crisis for ten years. Greece, Portugal, Ireland, Spain and Cyprus were unable to meet their debt repayments without assistance from the European Central Bank, the International Monetary Fund, or other Euro zone countries. Unemployment in Greece and Spain reached more than one it four (27%) while nearly half of the younger population was unemployed. Economic growth in the Euro zone has been muted, and in some places like Italy, there has been no growth for a decade. Again, the Euro zone economy is growing; but that does not mean it is in good shape. The strains are obvious. The currency has only lasted this long because of the huge political capital invested in the 'ever closer union' idea. That might sound good to the project leaders in Brussels, but the EU public is not so sure.

Such turmoil in the Western world has fed the nationalist argument that 'foreigners are taking our jobs', and calls to restrict immigration.

Throughout Europe, in Turkey, Austria, Italy, Germany and even closer to home, nationalists are in the ascendant, threatening to close their countries to foreign goods and foreign people. We've seen all kinds of people and parties challenging, and sometimes supplanting, mainstream politics. We've seen Donald Trump, Bernie Sanders, Alexandria Ocasio-Cortez in the US; Jeremy Corbyn and Brexit in the UK; a Socialist Green being elected as Prime Minister in Iceland; other Green parties advancing elsewhere; separatism in Catalonia, Alex Salmond and Nicola Sturgeon's Scottish National Party; Geert Wilders' Party for Freedom in the Netherlands, Jörg Meuthen and Alexander Gauland's Alternative für Deutschland in Germany, Beppe Grillo's Five Star Movement and the Lega Nord forming a coalition in Italy, Norbert Hofer's Freedom Party in Austria, Jimmie Akesson's Sweden Democrats Andrej Babis's ANO (Action of Dissatisfied Citizens) in the Czech Republic, and Marine Le Pen's National Front in France — ultimately defeated by another newcomer, Emmanuel Macron (and even he thinks that, given half a shot, his countrymen would vote for Frexit).

Back in the UK, meanwhile, extreme socialism has zombied back from the dead, replacing moderates in national and local government by hard-liners who bully and intimidate opponents and have captured the leadership of the Labour Party. The national debate has revived zombie policies long thought dead and buried: nationalisation of transport, utilities and banks, tougher regulation, higher taxes (on 'the rich', or someone, but definitely not you in the audience), huge rises in public spending (including that £500bn on infrastructure), more borrowing, controls on capital, caps on rents and fares and anything else you care to name, a £10 minimum wage (or maybe £15, who's counting?), plus all sorts of other ideas that have been tried before, to destruction. Yes, it is a good time to stay sharp, to be streetwise.

The ruling mob

The established politicians and parties have controlled the neighbourhood for so long, however, that they have got out of the habit of being streetwise. So they freeze like rabbits caught in the headlights. The right-thinking intellectuals sneer at the stupidity and coarseness of the new nationalist challengers and the Leave voters. The mainstream media cannot believe that a new 'populism' or radical socialism can seriously threaten our grand liberal institutions.

But they are all part of the cosy cartel that has run our political and economic neighbourhood for so long. Absorbed in their own world and its personalities, views and processes, they cannot understand what is going on because they do not realise how far they have jettisoned liberal democracy and replaced it with their own control-freak liberal autocracy — what the leading British journalist Allister Heath calls 'managerialism'. The millions of ordinary people who are discomfiting that managerialist mafia know exactly what they are doing. They think that our politicians should represent us, defend us, and guarantee our rights and freedoms. In return, we should give them the power to do that. But instead, these well-educated and well-connected public guardians have become convinced that they know better than we do what is good for us. And they abuse their power to impose those opinions on us. They do not realise that ordinary people do not want to be managed and told what to think, and say, and do. That is why voters are seeking to unnerve the managerialists and take back control of their own lives.

The Brexit Referendum result may have been close in percentage terms, but with over 33 million votes cast and 17,410,742 of them pro-Leave, it was still the largest popular mandate in British history. In a general election, the majority would have been a landslide. The subsequent, strenuous efforts of MPs, Peers, media commentators and intellectuals to thwart the result, says Heath, illustrates how "their contempt for real democracy is matched only by their preposterous self-regard." He might also have cited EU officials' haughty disdain for Brexit and their refusal to ease the process, or the earlier overturning of Irish and Danish referendums that rejected EU treaties. But to the managerialists of both Left and Right, "popular voting is fine as long as it doesn't change anything."

And why should the managerialist mafia want anything to change? They have it pretty good. They have the power to impose their worldview on the rest of us. They have the money, forcibly extracted from taxpayers, to make their social dreams come true— and to give favours to their cronies in politics and business. Indeed, the larger that government grows, the more money and patronage they control. It is hard, even for the most public-spirited, not to be seduced. But the result of this self-indulgence is a general public that sees politicians as being in office only to benefit themselves, and despises them for it.

The public have come to despise the officials, economists and authorities that shore up this managerialist state too. Officials are seen as no longer there to uphold principles, but as henchmen put there to push through the politicians' schemes, hassle those with no power to resist, bring in as much tax as possible, and pay out benefits as grudgingly as possible. Economists and central bankers have obsessed so much on the detail of economic management and regulation that they seem to have missed the big picture. While Gordon Brown's shiny new Financial Services Authority fixated on things like how quickly banks picked up the phone to their customers, they did not spot that the whole system was coming apart. "Why did nobody see this coming?" said the Queen as she visited the London School of Economics soon after the 2008 financial crash. The LSE's finest stared silently at their moccasins.

The Godfathers of the state

The managerialist mafia that controls the political-economic neighbourhood is a cartel of all kinds of people, all well educated and all convinced that they know how our lives should be run. They include politicians and economists, civil servants, broadcasters, academics, public intellectuals and others. Most owe their living to the state in some form: they may work directly in local or national government, in healthcare or education; they may work in sectors such as broadcasting, the law and other professions that are heavily controlled by the state; or they may work for trade unions, lobbyists and others who are deeply involved in and reliant on the political process. The majority will be products of a very few elite state-run universities, where many will have studied managerialist subjects such as politics and economics, under managerialist-minded professors whose library shelves groan under the weight of Marxian critiques of capitalism.

These Godfathers of the state see themselves as uniquely qualified to talk about and run things because of their intellect, education, urbanity, sensitivity and moderation. They reinforce each other in the supposed correctness of their views. They are genuinely shocked when members of the public deviate from their world view, putting it down to stupidity, coarseness, or extremism. After I outlined the case for Brexit, for example, one Cambridge academic told me: "You are the first sentient person I've heard with those views." Presumably either nobody else had ever penetrated her ivory prejudice bubble, or she regarded anyone who had as less than *sapiens*.

This urbane, metro-managerialist mafia, comfortably cushioned by education, position, state power, taxpayer money and the admiration of their peers, run our lives, but are not part of them. Rather, they shape and amend public affairs in their own image, and for their own comfort and benefit. They hardly even realise that they are doing so, being wholly focused on the world of their own creation, and convinced that it is the only decent, possible and sustainable one. They do not realise that most of the rest of us live in a different world, with different values.

Unlike the real outside world, the managerialists' world is unchanging. They see things as driven, not by individuals but by groups and the state, which never die. In this static world, rich people stay rich, unless the government intervenes to share out their good fortune with others; poor people stay poor, unless the government does something to relieve them; big businesses stay big, so must be curbed; and small firms stay small, so can be ignored. It is a world built on mechanisms, not motivations. Higher taxes always bring higher revenues: no thought is given to the possibility of people simply downing tools or leaving the country in response. Government regulation and spending always achieves its aims: again, scant thought is given to the possibility of wider, unanticipated, damaging consequences.

It is a managed world, a world devoid of dynamism, of risk-taking, of surprises, of entrepreneurship, of the enterprise and effort that enables poor individuals to become rich and small firms to grow big, of the natural ability of individuals to provide for themselves without being assisted or instructed by the state, and of people with motivations of their own that can and do thwart the best intentions of regulators and planners. Not surprisingly, therefore, the managerialists' policy prescriptions are equally devoid of anything that promotes creativity or dynamism, focusing only on managing the imagined stasis. By contrast, the streetwise public, not so cushioned, cocooned and self-pampered, are fully aware that life is in flux and that success does not come easily — and is easily knocked off course by events, particularly by the inept policies of a distant class that does not even understand ordinary life.

It is worse than that, however. Much of the public policy that comes out of this media-political class is not merely inept, but downright criminal. The street mafia might extort money from you by holding a gun to your head or threatening to burn down your business, but that is nothing compared to the managerialist mafia's power to arrest you, prosecute you, fine you, throw you in jail, revoke your trading licences or trash you and your reputation in the media. The mob's numbers rackets is a kids' game compared to the managerialists' Ponzi scheme of a state pension — from which the poor do much worse than the rich simply because the rich live longer. Loan sharking isn't a patch on our managerialist governments' ability to obliterate your savings through inflation. Drugs? Well, the managerialist mafia has a monopoly on what medicines you can access, and decides for you what you are and are not allowed to put into your body (even fatty foods). Gambling? The National Lottery collects money from large numbers of mostly poorer people, and puts it towards projects that the managerial class approves of. Firearms? The police have come to be armed, without any public debate on the matter, so do not imagine you can challenge the managerialists with impunity. Mafia laundries? In health, education and many other important parts of life, you simply cannot escape using the political mafia's monopolies — unless you can afford to pay for the privilege.

You might be able to escape the urban mafia by moving out of town, but you cannot escape the pervasive power of the managerialist state. Self-assertive, self-assured and armed with the keys to the local jail, it has come to drain freedom out of every part of your waking life. Nobody intended that: it is just the way that our so-called democracy has worked out. So now, your schooling, your healthcare, the conditions under which you work, rules about your personal relationships, the shape of public services of every kind, your money, your property, your savings, even entertainment and sport — nothing escapes the political mafia's attention and intervention. It tells you what you can and cannot say, and what you can and cannot do, right down to deciding the size of your fizzy pop bottle or telling you the number of calories you should eat each day. And it taxes or bans anything that does not meet its approval.

The public response

No wonder, then, that people are falling into the arms of those who promise an escape. No wonder that, in country after country, a whole array of political movements — nationalists, socialists, anarchists, you name it — have come along to offer the public every variety of such alternatives. As indeed have others that one can only describe as anti-political movements, like Brexit, or Catalonian separatism. No wonder that people are grasping for new and radical economic alternatives. And when ordinary people, revolted by the prissy complacency and self-absorption of the managerialist class, get their information instead from the badlands of Twitter, it is also no wonder that it is the high-profile anti-establishment mavericks that capture their consciousness. Hence the prominence of Jeremy Corbyn, of any number of nationalists in Continental Europe, of Bernie Sanders and Donald Trump.

People do not vote *for* politicians as much as vote *against* them. That is particularly true of younger people, who have long since given up on mainstream news, and who feel most acutely that public policy is shaped for the benefit of old, rich insiders. They are right: look no further than the pensions 'triple lock' and all the other benefits given to pensioners — free TV licences, free bus travel, free NHS prescriptions, Winter Fuel Payments, lower National Insurance rates and all the rest — by which politicians help pensioners (already one of the wealthiest groups in society) to say wealthy, simply because they are more likely to vote than other people.

But then, like death, Corbyn, Sanders & Co hold no terrors for the young—nor indeed for many others who are sick of mainstream politicians. Four in ten Americans now say they prefer socialism—the tie-dyed-red-in-the-wool socialism of the likes of Bernie Saunders—to capitalism. Many young people in the UK (though fewer than is claimed) voted for the still more doctrinaire socialist Jeremy Corbyn. It seems that the ideology that killed—who knows, 140 million people, give or take ten million or so?—is popular again. But then few people under the age of 40 remember the horrors of socialism. (Not even Stalin or Mao called it 'communism' as Westerners tend to do. They saw their 'socialism' as just the start of the process by which full communism would be achieved—a prospect which must flutter the heart of any Corbyn supporter.) A third of under-35s have never even heard of Mao, never mind the genocidal maniac Pol Pot. They think that George Bush's Middle East wars killed more than Stalin. But with the Berlin Wall now demolished, the obscene reality of what lay behind is now all too clear.

And yet Corbyn and Sanders seem such *nice* socialists. Quite charming, in Corbyn's case. Human. Avuncular. Good with school groups, coffee mornings, that sort of thing. Dedicated, visionary but (as Douglas Adams's *The Hitchhiker's Guide To The Galaxy* would put it) mostly harmless. As a result, people are willing to overlook the ideology (and the flaky regimes and causes) that he defends and the thuggish groups that promoted him into power. With relief and enthusiasm, they see him as potentially saving us from a distant ruling class—though they think less about what new oppression his ideology might unleash. And given the state power available to those elected to wield it, that is taking a life-threatening risk.

No doubt about it: there are powerful and dangerous forces, movements, groups and people around in today's bleak political and economic environment. You need to keep your wits about you. To understand what is going on and how things really work.

You need to be streetwise.

HOW WE GOT INTO THIS MESS

2 The rise of the managerialist state

A murder of upstart crows

Sometimes the movements that now challenge managerialist politics have a positive agenda. They crystallise the public's desire for less insider cronyism and more focus on the problems of ordinary people. And they advance constitutional and policy proposals to repair a broken political system.

More often, they have no positive agenda—or they focus on just one issue—aiming only to reflect the widespread public discontent and give voice to the less vocal voters' rage against their rulers. This is not necessarily a defect: it is good for complacent leaders to have their prejudices challenged. Early on, the UK Independence Party (UKIP) was this sort of movement, focusing only on Brexit. As it picked up support, however, the managerialists pressed UKIP on where it stood on other issues. It was a clever move: UKIP's clear Brexit message became clouded with populist policies on crime, migration and other issues, allowing the establishment to swat them away as merely 'an upstart crow, beautified with our feathers,' as the Cambridge-educated author Robert Greene said of the country-boy William Shakespeare. And yet, UKIP succeeded in its aim of getting a Brexit referendum, and winning it, much to the consternation of the managerialists.

In country after country, there now seems no shortage of upstart crows, not all of them as wholesome as UKIP. There are demagogues, parties and pressure groups that talk in anti-managerialist terms but have their own agenda that is often no less illiberal, cronyist and statist than the cliques they want to overturn. They are routinely branded as 'Far Right', but you need to be streetwise about such language. It might suggest that these groups must be against everything that the 'Far Left' (and even moderates) support—state control of industry, banks and public services, for example, or protectionism and state welfare. But the reality is often the reverse: they want all that and more. The Left are their opponents only because their agendas are so similar. They share the Far Left's disdain for the current system of representative democracy. They draw attention to real and imagined social and economic inequalities (often blaming migration and the favoured treatment of minorities). They have a revolutionary zeal and confidence in the correctness of their opinions. Many are perfectly willing to promote policies that benefit only their own supporters, to censor opponents, and use force to get their way. They are equally authoritarian, equally willing to subjugate civil liberties and individual rights to their own vision of society. The street thugs deployed in support of some of the wilder 'Far Right' parties in Eastern Europe and beyond seem little different from the militant Far Left street thugs who in the 2017 UK General Election threatened, abused and intimidated candidates, councillors and voters who opposed Jeremy Corbyn and Momentum's chosen allies. The 'cyber nats' of the Scottish National Party conducted equally vicious online campaigns against those prepared to oppose their view, or even those who — like the *Harry Potter* author JK Rowling — simply sought a more open debate. But the SNP certainly does not regard itself as 'Far Right'. Indeed, they came to dominate the Parliament in Holyrood by being further to the Left than Scottish Labour.

It is not so much a Left-Right spectrum as a horseshoe, or maybe a circle. After all, 'Nazi' is simply a shortening of National German Socialist Workers' Party, and the party's rhetoric was all about working-class social solidarity, the evils of capitalist 'exploitation' and managing the economy for the common benefit. Sure, they were vicious, militaristic racist murderers too, but you cannot plausibly dismiss the *Socialist Workers* bit merely as a branding exercise to cloak their real but less attractive agenda. They invested far too much in the reality that the *Socialist Workers* brand encapsulated.

Still, whatever the truth of that (and the debate on it continues), it remains true that many of today's upstart crows would like nothing better than to replace the existing politics with their own prejudices, and create governments that would be no more open, and no less interfering, commanding and statist than today's. One can see it in Donald Trump's American nationalism, his populism, and his protectionist measures aimed, among other things, at making the US steel industry great again (even in a world where the US cannot actually make the specialist steel it needs, and never could make it at a viable cost). Bernie Sanders and Jeremy Corbyn and their colleagues may argue furiously against everything the establishment stands for, and talk of liberating the forgotten and downtrodden, but they are certainly not advocates of rolling back the state. Like them, many supposedly 'Far Right' parties are just as controlling, in the name of 'national' objectives – that is, their own particular vision of the nation's objectives. As in George Orwell's *Animal Farm*, you can look from pig to man, and man to pig, but it is hard to tell much difference.

Origins of the managerialist state

So how did we end up with a political and economic system that is so detached from the everyday world of ordinary citizens that it has come under such assault from the good, the bad and the downright ugly?

Perhaps it was ever thus. The complacent, patrician, class-based establishment politics of the Edwardian era were maybe not so different. And it had its own radical ('anarchist') critics. But today's new managerialists are worse. They are not identifiable by top hats and wing collars. Indeed, they strive to look just like the people they represent, and pretend to share their interest in sport, television and much else, even while nursing their own superiority. They are as self-serving as any Edwardian patrician; but unlike the Edwardians, they can draw upon two-fifths of the nation's income to finance their patronage. They may not all be born into an elitist class (even though many learn their elitism in our posher schools and universities), but they still regard their own judgement as superior and more enlightened than those of the masses. That is why, for example, they were disgusted by the Brexit vote, and searched so strenuously for ways to reverse it – not by another referendum of the stupid unwashed, of course, but by the Parliament of themselves and their peers.

The new cartels

Today's managerialism is a cartel of mutually supporting mobs: not just the political and economic mafia, but the media too. The Left love to attack Rupert Murdoch, even though his alleged media dominance is a pinprick compared to the monopoly power of the BBC. But it is due to him that we now have 24-hour television news and current affairs. With Sky TV, he pioneered satellite broadcasting, which made possible huge numbers of new channels, including a 24-hour news and current affairs channel. It was soon mimicked by the BBC with its own 24-hour News Channel, then by others. And between them, these channels changed the nature of politics. After all, 24 hours is a lot of broadcast time to fill — day, after day, after day — which means creating or buying in huge amounts of content.

The thing about news, of course, is that while it might be interesting to hear about tsunamis in the Far East, what really grabs UK viewers is news about the UK, or about what events elsewhere mean for people in the UK. So, as a broadcaster, you cannot just buy stock news items from abroad, as you might do with documentaries or cartoons or sitcoms. To keep news relevant to your customers, you have to do it yourself. That means finding a lot of what television producers extravagantly call 'talent' — reasonably articulate people who can go on camera and talk about issues in terms of what they mean for the UK public.

It might seem an oxymoron to call politicians 'talent', but they are keener than anyone to help the broadcasters out. For a start, most of them are shameless prima donnas. It is said that politics is merely acting for people who can't get a job on stage: these failed actors are very pleased to strut on camera. Second, they are so confident in the superiority of their own views that they are always keen to give them to us. And third, they want to get their spin on events into the public domain before anyone else has the opportunity to gainsay them.

This third point is why, when ministers want to advertise some new policy, they no longer bother with the traditional courtesy of informing MPs first. Instead they leak it to the media. Of course, they will swear that they intended to make the announcement in

Parliament, but that the naughty media had somehow got hold of it first. But everyone knows that such leaks give ministers the opportunity to present each announcement — to spin it — in the most glowing terms. And as party colleagues will have been briefed in advance, they can pitch themselves to television and radio stations and polish up that glow even more. The broadcasters, meanwhile, are delighted to get the scoop, and happy to let them spin, in the hope of getting yet more. So before Opposition MPs are even out of bed, the new policy has received such a rapturous welcome that it then becomes hard to criticise it. But if the minister had simply stood up in the House of Commons and announced the government's intentions, the idea would have been torn to shreds by the Opposition and the government's own dissidents even before the story was written.

So politicians need the media to boost themselves and their policies, while the broadcasters (and print journalists, who are now expected to write more and more online as well as their newspaper pieces) need the politicians to fill their slots and to give them early scoops about impending announcements. Indeed, as the number of channels has multiplied, so has the urgency of getting scoops. The politicians play the media by giving different scoops to one, then another, then another — which leaves all of them sucking up to ministers, and giving them easy rides in return for exclusives. It is a very neat symbiosis. The power of elected leaders is boosted, the media gain importance, and the media-political cartel expands its influence yet wider. The streetwise viewer, listener or reader must look behind the headlines: more important is how and why the cartel creates them.

Regulation has helped to make this convenient media-political symbiosis possible. The protections of copyright, patents and intellectual property has allowed giant media groups to consolidate, with little fear of competition. One sees it with Microsoft, Apple, Google and Facebook, but also with satellite and cable broadcasting. Indeed, the regulations that were supposed to promote the cabling of the UK, and give people much more choice in television channels, simply helped Sky. Back in the 1980s, colleagues and I in Westminster decided we should have cable television. The only snag was that the law gave a single company a monopoly on installing the cable. And the company — true to the nature of a monopoly — told us that it while it was indeed scheduled to cable our patch, it had no plans to start any time soon. Could we get satellite, then? No, we could not install a satellite dish in an area that was scheduled to be cabled — even if there was no cable and scant prospect of one soon. So we went ahead and installed the satellite dish anyway. Sky probably did very well out of the fact that people were not getting the cabling they expected. The result of all the 'helpful' and 'liberalising' legislation was to create two monopolies, one in cable and the other in satellite.

Professionalising the gangs

The next big factor that has driven a wedge between the public and their leaders is the 'professionalisation' of politics and politicians. It was never intended, but the political process itself helped create it. For centuries, the hours of the House of Commons were framed deliberately to allow MPs to have a second job. Not much happened until 2:30pm. Contentious business did not start until later still. There would be a vote at 7:00pm, and then another at 10:00pm, so that MPs could go off for dinner in between, leaving just a handful of colleagues to man the façade. Thanks to these hours, many MPs were able to spend their mornings working privately. Quite a few were lawyers, appearing in London's law courts for most of the day, popping back in the late afternoon for a little brightener in one of the Palace of Westminster's many bars, before trooping through the lobby and out to dinner. There was never much business on a Friday, and nothing very controversial on a Thursday, so MPs could nurse their constituencies and their businesses back home. And of course the holidays (genteelly called 'recesses') were generously long.

Some campaign groups thought that this was a bit of a con. They argued that taxpayers were forking out MPs' salaries (around £63,000pa at the time, three times more than the average citizen could hope to earn) yet their MPs were not devoting anything like their full time to the job of serving those taxpaying constituents. Also, parliamentary hours were very bad for female MPs, many of whom were looking after children and wanted to spend evenings with their families rather than having to hang around Westminster, sometimes until midnight and beyond, for the sole purpose of going through whichever lobby the whips herded them into.

For this mixture of reasons, the hours of the House of Commons were revised. Committee work (which was of growing importance, given the complexity of modern legislation) would occupy MPs in the morning, and the other serious business would be done in the afternoon, making it more of a nine to five job (though in the event, the evening sessions still go on until 10:00pm). So MPs mostly scaled down their outside work, or abandoned it entirely. New MPs either gave up their business or professional careers once elected, or never embarked on one in the first place.

The result of all this is that politics is no longer a matter of public service, but a career in itself. If you go to Mount Vernon, George Washington's home outside the US capital, you find that it was a working farm. Go into the house itself and you see that the pictures, the plasterwork, even the furniture show bucolic scenes, sheaves of wheat, horns of plenty, and all the other things that remind you that you are in the country, working the land. It makes visitors realise, as Dan Hannan MEP once observed, that this was the home of a man who, in later life, would trudge up to the capital to serve his country and make its laws — but then could not wait to get home to his real job as a farmer.

Today, though, there are precious few MPs with any experience outside politics. We have inadvertently created a Parliament stuffed full of career politicians. Their apprenticeship for the job is not about showing their abilities in real business or professional life, but in proving their political credentials. They start in student politics and campaigns. They get elected to the local council. They join campaign groups, or — like former PM David Cameron — work for PR agencies (where they are schmoozing politicians all the time) or trade unions. They move on by fighting one or two 'bad' seats that nobody expects them to win, where they learn campaigning skills. Then it is on to a 'safe' seat and into Parliament. Next it is a committee appointment, or maybe serving as a junior whip. Then

Parliamentary Private Secretary (i.e. bag carrier) to a minister. From there they hope to become a Parliamentary Under Secretary (junior minister), then a Minister of State (senior minister), then—who knows?—Privy Counsellor, Secretary of State and a seat in Cabinet. Then on to the Lords.

And there are vast numbers of these Parliamentary appointments. Out of a House of Commons of 650 MPs, roughly 100 are part of 'the government'. On the Opposition benches are another 100 'shadows' who hope to step into those government jobs. Then on each side there are another 100 or so who would *like* to be filling those government and shadow positions. So out of 650 MPs, about 400 are pursuing their own political careers, leaving a minority of 250 or so to actually represent the public.

The House of Commons Library, which is Parliament's independent research team, found that in 1980, around 45% of MPs were professionals such as lawyers, doctors or teachers. By 2010 it was 35% and falling. Meanwhile, the number of career politicians, with no real experience in business or the professions, rose from around 3% to 15% in the same period. The trend continues: at the 2015 election, around one in four (26%) of new candidates were professional politicians, policy advisers, researchers, party officers, trade unions or lobbyists. The party with most of these insiders on its candidates list was the Scottish National Party (a whopping 47%). Nearly a quarter (23%) of Labour candidates in 2015 worked for trade unions. More than half (53%) of the Liberal Democrats who stood in the general election were local councillors, as were two-fifths (43%) of SNP candidates. The greatest number of apparatchiks are found in the marginal 'swing' seats, where parties prefer insiders they know (and can control). So much for Abraham Lincoln's government 'by the people'.

Paying the mobsters

There are other reasons why Parliament attracts ever more career politicians. An MP's basic salary, at just over £77,000, is not a huge amount of money, given the responsibility of the job. It is much less than a comparable job would pay in industry. (You might think that this is a false comparison, because many MPs would be incapable of holding down a proper job, but that is a separate issue.) True, there is also a pension plan that the rest of us can only dream of, and you never have to worry about paying for breakfast, lunch, afternoon tea or dinner ever again; but some of that is true of other executive jobs. The money that MPs get remains comparatively modest.

But then there is never a good time for MPs to raise their own pay. Even though the public expect MPs to work round the clock for them, most people still earn far less than their MP, and it looks bad if the difference becomes too wide. So while countless reports have called for MPs' salaries to be raised, they are raised only cautiously – the aim being to avoid headlines about fatcat MPs snoozing on the leather benches (or not being in the chamber at all) while taxpayers slave.

And hence, in turn, the expenses scandal. The deal was quite simple. Putting up parliamentary salaries always brings complaints. So instead (wink, wink), we will just provide very generous expenses, which nobody will notice. Need to have a home in the constituency? Buy yourself a house, call it your principal home, and do it up on expenses. Need to stay over in Westminster? Buy yourself another house, call that your principal home, and do it up on expenses. Need to drive places – or even cycle? There are generous expenses for that too. Buying tea and biscuits for the constituents? No problem, every Jaffa Cake can be claimed. Anything else you need…?

It was all going so well until the *Daily Telegraph* revealed the corruption of it all. The duck houses, the flipping the home trick, it was all there. And as well as the questionable, there was the downright illegal – like the fake receipts submitted by Denis MacShane, which got him a six-month jail sentence. He wasn't the only one. Though I did feel sorry for a few MPs, like Douglas Carswell, whose expenses were very modest and down to earth, but included a 'love seat' that the press had a good laugh over. "I wish I had spent more, like everyone else, and got a sofa instead," he said, ruefully. And of course there was Douglas Hogg, who – being a busy chap – simply handed the parliamentary authorities a list of his household expenses and asked them to pay whatever was claimable. Sadly the list included the cost of clearing the moat round his manor house, which had the effect of solidifying the public view that the political class lived in a completely different, privileged and bizarre world.

They are not far wrong. Politics no longer attracts people who want to contribute something to public life and then return to a proper job. It attracts those whose lives and careers are politics. And the only way to succeed in this competitive profession is to start young, rejecting real-world career paths and getting yourself on the political track. After a lifetime in (mostly publicly funded) political jobs, you will not know anything about how businesses work, or how to read a set of accounts, or industrial relations, or risk and taxes and bankruptcy; but you might get to be a minister and deliver to the nation your own opinions about such things.

This dangerous neighbourhood

With politics now a lifetime career in its own right—not just for MPs but for the wider political class that includes journalists, broadcasters, think tankers, advisers, public affairs consultants, trade unions, campaign groups and all the rest—there are plenty of people around who have come to believe that the world of politics is the best thing since spaghetti hoops. Even the least streetwise elector knows this is untrue, so instead the line becomes that 'democracy' is wonderful, and that we should decide more things 'democratically'. Democracy is a good thing: who could object to more of it?

But what the political class mean by saying that more things should be decided 'democratically' is that more things should be decided *politically*—by them and through the political process they are part of. By this sleight of hand, more and more decisions over people's quotidian existence come to be made through the political process, rather than by individuals themselves.

Unfortunately the remorseless expansion of the political process in the name of 'democracy' generates more decisions and more work than any individual can possibly monitor. MPs cannot even read the heaps of law and regulation that they sign off, never mind understand it or contemplate its likely consequences. Politicians become too busy to think. They become mere managers of the political process, hoping for little more than to hold things together. No longer visionaries, nor even informed representatives, they end up as mere managers, trying to hold their political establishment together. Soon the public come to question what they are there for, beyond their own status and enrichment. And new political gangs are formed to take them down.

It pays to be streetwise in this dangerous neighbourhood.

3 The rise of politics

Seeds of its own destruction

The alienated millions who vote for Trump, or Brexit, or the Far Right or Far Left populist parties, are not just voting against particular managerialist politicians. They are protesting against an entire political system that they see as rigged against them — which it is. Nobody intended representative democracy to morph into unrepresentative managerialism, but that is its nature. It carries within it, as Karl Marx said, the seeds of its own destruction. Political office attracts precisely those you would not want holding it — those with a little learning, who believe they know best how people should live, and who are prepared to use the power of the state to make them. As the American author William F Buckley put it, "I would rather be governed by the first 2,000 people in the Boston telephone directory than by the 2,000 people on the faculty of Harvard University." Even worse, our political system attracts those — such as pressure groups, lobbyists, political parties, demagogues and the media — who know how to use the system, and its shortcomings, in their own interest. If you are streetwise, you know that things are in need of very profound reform.

I used to think that politics was a process of rational argument. People would advance different arguments about what needed to be done, and our political representatives would consider it and debate it, before coming to an informed conclusion on the matter. Yes, there would be different parties with different starting positions on many subjects, but once all the arguments had been aired, the public interest could be identified and the laws created to serve it.

That was naïve. I realised just how naïve when I worked for a group of Representatives in the US Congress. One day I was tasked with skimming through that year's Farm Bill. The first four-fifths of this monster document dealt with various rural concerns, though it was mostly about giving grants, favours, privileges and subsidies to America's farmers — an important and influential lobby group. The end fifth was about Food Stamps, a welfare programme to give needy families free vouchers that they could exchange for food in shops and supermarkets. It struck me as odd that what was obviously a welfare measure should be tacked on the end of a law about farming and rural affairs. Being new in Washington, I asked colleagues about this anomaly. They looked at me as if I had descended from Mars. "It's simple," they told me patiently. "Food Stamps go into the Farm Bill because all the Republicans, who represent rural farmers, vote for the farm subsidies, and all the Democrats, who represent city dwellers, vote for the welfare measure. So everyone's happy!" I had to reply that, while everyone in Washington might well be happy, I doubted that American taxpayers would be quite so enthusiastic. Suddenly, I realised that the political process – or a large and important part of it – had very little to do with the interests of the wider public, and a very great deal to do with the interests of particular interest groups and of the politicians who are in league with them. It was a dispiriting moment, but an educational and life-changing one. I was becoming politically streetwise.

Over the rest of that year in Washington, I saw the full range of the political games that so alienate the general public – the factionalism, the coalition building, the 'you vote for my measure and I'll vote for yours' tactics, the make-work jobs in Washington created for constituents, (such as the lift attendants in the Capitol's completely automatic lifts) the ploys to get jobs and federal spending into your own district, and all the over-governance that results from all these processes. I saw the lobby groups and the money they were prepared to spend on influencing legislators (and even their humble staffers: I was never short of free drinks and buffet food of an evening). It was indeed a swamp.

And yet managerialist intellectuals, of the Left in particular, still insist that democracy is a great system. If it has become corrupted, they say, that must be because we are not worthy of it. They blame our laziness in finding out about the issues, our apathy about voting, fake news, our shortsightedness and our parochialism. So keen are they to expand collective decision-making into more and more parts of life that they conveniently ignore the fact that democracy has always been corrupt, and exploited by those in charge. Go back as far as you like—the Corn Laws, say of 1815-1846, say, which were designed to protect farmers and landowners, at the expense of those who consumed cereals, and which took a great deal of political upheaval to repeal.

No, the problem is not that we have corrupted our democracy. The problem, as the streetwise observer knows, is that our democracy has corrupted us.

The fetishisation of democracy

Democracy is not actually the best system of making decisions, compared to all other systems. Nor is it even the least worst, as Winston Churchill once remarked. Rather, democracy is a passable way of making a very few decisions—the few decisions that we have to make and cannot make in other ways. For example, a popular vote is a reasonable way to decide on how we should defend and police ourselves. A few of my anarcho-capitalist friends would contest this, saying that private alternatives will provide all the security we need. But most people would say that defence is something we have to decide as a nation, and so whatever the majority choose is what we should go for. Or again, if there is disagreement about some infrastructure project—if it is widely thought that we need a new road, but nearby homeowners object, for example—it again seems reasonable to put the matter to a vote. Or if market forces seem unable to deliver a public good like clean air—as in the days when homes were heated by coal because it was cheap—then having a vote and passing a law seems to be an efficient way of achieving that objective.

The trouble is that we, and particularly our political leaders, fetishise democracy. If democracy is so absolutely wonderful at deciding all these great issues, they argue, then why not get democracy to decide a lot more? Like how our healthcare is managed? How our schools and universities are run? Or how our trains, buses and household utilities are provided? It is a beguiling idea: maybe such services *can* be run for the benefit of the public, rather than shareholders. Maybe they would be cheaper if they did not have to make profits and pay dividends. Maybe we could make sure that even the poorest were provided for if such things were decided democratically, rather than on the basis of profit.

Maybe — though as we now know from bitter experience in the 1960s and 1970s, maybe not. The trouble with this approach is that there is no obvious place to draw the line. We end up stretching democracy well beyond its capacity. And you cannot invoke democracy without politics coming along for the ride. What we call democratic decisions are really decisions that are made politically, through elections, legislative votes, and regulations. Which means that vital human services such as health, education and public services get dragged into politics. Everyone agrees that we should 'take politics out of healthcare' or 'take politics out of education', but if the running of health and education is left to democratic decision-making, that means they will always be subject to political debate, and therefore political disagreement, since disagreement is an inevitable, indeed healthy, part of democracy. You cannot complain about a vital service becoming a 'political football' if you have already thrown it onto the pitch.

Worse, the fetishisation of democracy sees democratic — that is, political — decisions working their way into every part of our lives, public or personal. Should the size of drinks cans or restaurant meals be limited by law in order to save us from obesity? Should we ban plastic bottles to save the planet? Should we be prevented from taking recreational drugs, even though the only person harmed, if any, would be us? Should we ban gambling or prostitution or smoking or shops opening on Sunday because the majority dislike them? Should we force people to pay higher taxes to pay for the opera, or the BBC, or public libraries, just because the majority in power think they are a good thing? And even if the majority do agree on such issues, what right do they have to force their opinions (and the cost of those opinions) onto the minority? If we really believe that the majority are always right and that their views should prevail, there is no limit to what decisions are made politically — no end to the tyranny that the majority can exert over other people's lives.

That is a sure way to give democracy a bad name. And the creeping politicisation of life, the creeping enforcement of the managerialists' opinions on the rest of us, is an important reason why ordinary people have become so bloody-minded at the polls. The solution, however, is not to replace one set of politicians with another, potentially even more oppressive, set. The only way to redeem democracy is to limit it to those few decisions that we cannot actually make for ourselves. And that is not many.

How democracy works (or doesn't)

Literally, 'democracy' means 'rule by the people'. But in fact it is not (and never has been) the people who make all of the decisions, it is their representatives in the legislature. We have a *representative* democracy. Why should that be? Should we not *all* take a careful interest in what decisions are made over our lives? A noble ambition: but streetwise observers know that, in reality, most of us have much better things to do than to sit around debating the finer points of some arcane law or regulation. How many of us really care about (or are even qualified to talk about) sewerage provision in Shetland, civil service pay rates, fire standards in grain silos, or the taxation of offshore bonds? We all have plenty of our own concerns to worry about—rounding up chums for an evening in the pub, planning a weekend trip, painting the bedroom, fixing the car, finding a better job, patching up things with the relatives, checking out the best value hairdryers, going to the football, snuggling down with the latest *Game of Thrones*, and much more. That is why representative government is a businesslike division of labour. Ordinary people do all the interesting things, and we elect some poor nerds to do the Shetland sewerage stuff.

Put that way, it sounds like a pretty rotten job, and perhaps it should be: something that people do out of public duty, but with no great relish. Yet there is never any shortage of people willing to do the job—which is a worrying sign straight away. Certainly, a few people might stand for elected office because they genuinely want to help their fellow citizens and believe they have the ability to make a positive difference. Many might stand in order to improve the lot of their own group, class, gender or other interests.

Sadly, most MPs stand because politics is their whole life, because they love power and celebrity, and because they think they know how everyone's lives should be run. And even if their original motivations were more public-spirited, the joy of being in the thick of it soon overwhelms them.

The theory of representative democracy is that, instead of trying to become experts on every policy issue ourselves, we elect specialist practitioners to do that specialist job—just as we hire doctors to cure us, rather than trying to become experts on medicine. We elect people to represent our views in the debate on these issues. And more than that, we elect people whose judgement we think might well be better than ours because they have the time to understand complex issues, and the experience and expertise to decide sensibly on them. "Your representative," wrote the great eighteenth-century politician Edmund Burke, owes you, not his industry only, but his judgement; and he betrays instead of serving you if he sacrifices it to your opinion."

Streetwise electors, knowing how power corrupts, would prefer to be far more specific about what they want to leave to their representatives' judgement—or not. But there are darn few streetwise electors, for the same reason: we all have far too much to do than to bother about the who's who and who supports what of election campaigns. Though most people can recognise photographs of the Prime Minister and Leader of the Opposition, for example, public recognition of other ministers tails off markedly. Some Cabinet members are lucky if even one in ten people know who they are. And as for which parties promote which policies, polls reveal that most people simply do not have a clue.

But why should people bother? Though we are urged (by politicians) to 'use our democratic right to vote', the fact is that someone's vote makes precious little difference to events. Most constituencies in the UK are 'safe' seats for one party or another. Only in a few 'swing' seats is there any real chance of removing or electing a particular candidate. And hardly ever is an MP (or even a local councillor, where the number of voters is far less) elected on the strength of a single vote. It is literally millions to one. You have more chance of being run over on your way to the polling station than your vote making a difference in a General Election. True, your vote might give some tiny encouragement to the candidate you support, rather like cheering at a football match. But your vote will have even less influence on the result than your cheering.

Electors may not be completely streetwise, but they know when they are being conned. All that 'democratic right' stuff doesn't wash with them. They know that precious little will change, whatever they do. Even if their vote did make a one-in-many-millions difference, it would merely elect one kind of managerialist politician rather than another. So they conclude — perfectly rationally — that there is no point in boning up on the personalities and the issues in an election. Election campaigns can cover so many different subjects — both national issues like jobs, taxes, rising prices, defence, the health service, the EU or defence, and local issues like planning and schools — that the ordinary voter could not possibly become expert in all of them. And since your vote will not make a difference anyway, the rational action is to not to try. You might as well get on with your life and, if you plump for any candidate at all, do it on the basis of gut prejudice. Pour a beer, put your feet up, punch the TV zapper and skip over the election coverage to get to *Game of Thrones*, and revel in what economists call your *rational ignorance*. And if by chance you happen to catch politicians complaining about 'voter apathy', simply pour yourself another beer and change channels. It is the rational thing to do.

(Actually, if you *do* want to make a difference, that is not entirely the best advice. My usual procedure at elections is to spoil my ballot paper. Not just because voting simply encourages the managerialist political class, but because it is my one opportunity to send the managerialists a message. A 'spoilt' paper is any where the voter's intention is unclear, or one that might identify the voter — for example, any with handwriting on. At the count, the candidates gather round with the returning officer to go through the papers that have been designated as 'spoilt'. So, instead of putting a cross, or a number, against some candidate, if you write a message on your paper, all the candidates get to see it. It has to be a short message, because there are always many spoilt papers and they go through them quite quickly. But with a pithy phrase, you can get their attention. Get a couple of friends to do the same, and they think there is a groundswell of opinion. It might just change the way they act. Streetwise, or what?)

4 Troubleshooting democracy

The inevitable flaws

Giving absolute power to dictators is certainly asking for trouble. They are rarely benign—though Singapore's Lee Kuan Yew came close. They also rarely know when to quit—though much to the Left's discomfort, Augusto Pinochet not only turned round Chile's failing economy but also stepped down peacefully after a 1998 referendum on his leadership. And given the rational ignorance of voters, some form of *representative* democracy seems the only peaceful way of deciding the few things that we can only decide collectively. Sadly, democracy never confines itself to that modest task. Instead, our 'representatives' expand their decision-making into a vast array of things that we can and should decide for ourselves. And worse (as streetwise political economists know) the very process by which those decisions are made is deeply flawed, and unavoidably so.

Those are good reasons to keep democracy (i.e. politics) within limits. The American founding fathers made perhaps the world's best attempt to limit public decision-making to its essential role, to keep it out of private affairs, and to bind it with rules to prevent majorities bullying minorities and with checks to curb the abuse of power. Their constitution, a brilliant liberal document in some ways but a messy set of compromises in others, worked well until the Civil War, after which power became more centralised at the federal level. It became even more centralised in the New Deal era after the Wall Street Crash, when huge new federal agencies were created. The same trend continues even now: today's US government is larger, more centralised and more intrusive than ever.

One way to limit the sprawl of collective decision-making and protect the rights of minorities would be to make all such decisions unanimous. Then anyone could stop the majority usurping their rights. But that would make it difficult to reach unanimous agreement on almost anything. So for convenience, we tend to make decisions by a simple majority vote, where 50%+1 is enough to bind everyone.

Yet there is nothing magical about simple majorities. Indeed, for some things where we want to give minorities extra protection, we use qualified majority voting, such as a two-thirds rule. In the US, for example, if the President vetoes a bill, it can be reinstated only by a two-thirds 'supermajority' in the House and the Senate; and to ratify a foreign treaty requires a two-thirds majority in the Senate.

By contrast, nearly all political decisions in the UK — local and national elections, votes in Parliament, even referendums on the constitution — are made by simple majority. This is dangerous. For at every level — elections, lawmaking and the application of laws by officials — the public decision-making process is mired in the self-interest of those involved.

The gang war of interests

Start with elections. People think elections are about choosing people for office. In fact elections are about *removing* people from office. There is no shortage of people who enjoy power: power, as Lord Action didn't quite say, is delightful, and absolute power is absolutely delightful. And not many people give up power willingly. Take China's President Xi, who after a constitutional change can now stay in office indefinitely — which hardly demonstrates that China has ditched the old ways. Or President Putin of Russia, serving his terms, stepping down in favour of a placeman, and then returning and demanding an even longer stint. Or all those other dictators who lead their countries into years of destructive civil war rather than step down. At least democratic election allows leaders to be removed from power peacefully.

Of course, people do vote *for* their favourite candidates. But more important is who they vote *against*. Winston Churchill himself was ousted at the General Election of 1945 by an electorate that was tired of what he represented, namely, war. But did they all really want the radical, nationalising government of Clement Atlee, which ended in such chaos that the public decided to bring the ageing Churchill back? Or more recently, did most Americans really think that only the maverick Donald Trump could save them? Do those voting for oddball candidates in Germany or Italy really support all their strange policies? Did people in the UK really want Jeremy Corbyn as Prime Minister when so many voted Labour in 2017? Some, perhaps, but many more were simply sending a message that they'd had enough of managerialist politics.

The second mistake people make about elections is that they are tests of the national interest. There is no such thing as the national interest. Different people have diverse wants, needs, hopes and aspirations. They do not agree on how children should be schooled, how high taxes should be, how much should be spent on defence, healthcare, welfare or infrastructure. They each have *different* interests, and often *competing* interests. Should a new runway be built at London's Heathrow Airport? People who fly a lot might say yes, but people who live in the path of the bulldozers might say no. Should taxes be raised to pay for more welfare spending? Taxpayers might say no, poorer people might say yes. Should we have more defence, or spend the money on better policing? Should people have the right to speak freely, or should we ban racist language? Should we protect our own producers, or let customers buy cheaper goods from abroad? On countless such issues, there is no way of pleasing everyone. A decision that serves and pleases one group hurts another. In reality, therefore, elections are not a measure of 'the' public interest, but fight-outs between large numbers of different, conflicting interests, which are felt strongly, deeply and viscerally on each opposing side. That is why politics is the dirty business that it is.

It also explains the rise of lobbying, and the large effect that special interest groups have on elections. While many people feel strongly on one or two issues, nobody feels strongly on everything. Tomato growers, for example, might feel that they should be protected from the competition of foreign tomato growers. (Indeed, Italian tomato growers managed to hold up the proposed EU-Canada trade deal over this precise point.) So, whenever the opportunity arises, they will campaign vigorously for such protection, get other tomato growers to join them, form a lobby group, raise money to sponsor pro-tomato-protection candidates, and so on. Having such a specific interest, they are easily organised into a well-funded campaigning force. That is quite different from the situation of the general public. Few ordinary voters care whether there are quotas on the import of foreign tomatoes: home grown tomatoes may be more expensive, but it is a small item on their grocery bills. And who worries about where tomatoes come from anyway? The tomato lobby has a concentrated interest in this issue, while the general public has diffused interests.

The same is true for countless other issues. And that is the problem. Countless numbers of special interest groups, focused and well funded, have sprung up to exploit the electoral system. They can gain huge control over it, all the more so if they work together as a coalition: the tomato growers, the cauliflower cultivators, the pumpkin producers and the turnip farmers, all agreeing to pool money and campaign staff, and voting for each other's interests. Politicians appease such lobbies because they control many votes, and even the most public-spirited politicians (yes, they exist) need votes to get into office and do their good work. But if members of the general public have a position on vegetables at all, they are all over the place on it: what value are those disparate voters to a candidate?

As for the consequences of that, do the maths. If you can get a majority of 50%+1 for your party or coalition in just 50%+1 of the constituencies, then you have a 50%+1 majority in the legislature, and your special interest carries the day. Just over a quarter of the electorate is enough to get your policies into law — less, in reality, since many ordinary electors do not vote, giving you a clear run.

Godfather politics

These electoral realities have turned UK elections into presidential-style contests. Most people (quite rationally, as we have seen) know little about their local candidate. At most, they recognise the Prime Minister and Leader of the Opposition, and vote on whether they like them or not.

The growing importance of national television, and of 24-hour news, bolsters this trend. All some voters ever see of the campaign is the news headlines where the party leaders are interviewed, or the TV debates between them. (The debates were a crass constitutional mistake by David Cameron—since in the UK we do not elect a Prime Minister, but individual Members of Parliament. They were a crass political mistake too, because they allowed the third-party leader Nick Clegg to shine. And having conceded the 'leaders debate' principle, it is hard for any subsequent party leader to back out of them.)

The result of all this is that power is becoming increasingly concentrated in the party leaders, and Parliament comes to look more and more like the executive branch of government, rather than the legislative or representative branch. We should be electing MPs to restrain our leaders, but we have ended up electing leaders who then tell our MPs what to think.

So if you are truly streetwise, you know that elections are not the wonderful institutions they seem. It is no wonder that growing numbers of people are rejecting the whole political set-up.

The interests of the lawmakers

Once your local candidate has got into office, thanks to having an attractive party leader and sucking up to all the noisiest interest groups, what happens next? Well, your MP now has to promote legislation to pay off those debts to the interest-group coalitions. And they probably have other pet projects of their own to push through. To succeed, they will need to convince other MPs to support them. And those other MPs will want to extract favours in return. So deals are done, they walk through the division lobbies to support each others' measures and—like the Food Stamps measure tacked onto the Farm Bill—they end up passing more laws and regulations than anyone actually wants.

In fact, the logrolling, as the Americans call it, starts much earlier. Party manifestos are themselves the result of horse-trading between interests within the same party. Ministers bargain to get their own policies into the manifesto in return for supporting the policies of others: so everyone is pleased, except possibly the Chancellor, who has to find the money for it all. (An exception was the disastrous 2017 Conservative manifesto, which was written by two Downing Street policy wonks, and managed to please no one.)

There may even be another bout of horse-trading if the largest party is short of a majority and has to go into coalition pact with a smaller one. That can give the smaller party a huge influence on events, no matter how few voters it represents. In the 2010 Cameron-Clegg coalition negotiations, for example, the Liberal Democrats (with only 23% of the vote) were staggered at the generosity of what they were offered – including a referendum on proportional representation that could have seriously damaged the desperate Conservatives. And when the policy-wonk manifesto left Theresa May without a majority, she had to be equally generous to her coalition partners, the Democratic Unionist Party.

Even the simplest laws can morph into monsters when there are large numbers of interests to be bought off. An exquisite example is the 2008 emergency 'TARP' measure to bail out troubled US banks after the financial crash. When first presented to the US Congress it was just two pages long. But because it just had to pass, Members of Congress knew they could make all kinds of demands in exchange for their support. The Bill eventually emerged at 451 pages, and was full of horse-traded concessions: tax breaks for motorsports complexes and fishermen harmed by the Exxon Valdez oil spill, subsidies for people who cycle to work, $148m in tax reliefs for wool fabric producers, $192m in excise tax rebates for the rum industry, even a $2m tax benefit for makers of wooden arrows. Streetwise US taxpayers must have been less than thrilled.

The interests of the enforcers

To put these overblown, over-expensive laws into effect, you need enforcers – a bureaucracy of government officials, civil servants, agencies, departments, town halls, county halls, regulators, quangos and all the rest. Often they will need to promote additional regulations to patch over the gaps and ambiguities and make the laws work. Yet officials are not angels, any more than the politicians are. They may see themselves as having a vocation to serve the public, but they have their personal interests too. They may not deliberately let those interests influence how they do their job, but there is always a danger that they subconsciously tilt things towards their own satisfaction.

For a start, officials have an interest in making laws more complex than they need to be. To enforce the legislation consistently, they have to plug gaps and clarity uncertainties with additional rules and regulations—adding to the law's complexity. But also, the more complex the law is, the more officials are needed to interpret, implement and enforce it: and for senior officials, that means a bigger department, more status, influence and respect, and more money too.

Bureaucrats are also risk-averse: unlike entrepreneurs, who can potentially make themselves rich by taking risks, officials only lose by taking risks. If they let things go wrong, it reflects badly on them and their careers. So they spend a lot of time and taxpayer money on risk assessments, criminal records checks and much more. They impose the same risk-avoiding 'precautionary principle' rules on the public too, right down to the simplest Easter egg hunt. The police get in on the act, charging organisers for officers and equipment that is wholly disproportionate to the risks involved. The result is that public events become too expensive to stage, and people are denied the pleasure of getting together for some fun.

I saw bureaucratic risk-aversion in practice some years ago, when a new hospital in Norwich was put out to tender. Of course, the tender specifications grew and grew as each official threw in their own risk-avoiding demands. To meet all these concerns, one private consortium's bid was a pile of documents as tall as the boss was. It took two months for officials to come back with their first query: what kind of cutlery would be used in the canteen? You can see why public projects end up delayed and over-expensive. Even the Houses of Parliament, built around 150 years ago, came in three times over budget and 24 years late.

Then there are targets. Businesses have a clear measure of success: are they making a profit? But public services are not provided for profit; and without that simple indicator, officials have to make up targets for service quality, such as hospital waiting times, to gauge their performance. But of all the diseases that the National Health Service has to deal with, targetitis is the worst. Targets are why patients spend hours waiting in ambulances outside the hospital (the waiting-time clock does not start ticking until they have been 'admitted'). Through this and in many other ways, public services grow to be structured, not for the benefit of the public, but of administrators.

Complexity invites corruption. In Nepal you need something like two dozen different licences and permits to run a shop. But a report by the Samriddhi ('Prosperity') think tank showed that, of all the small businesses surveyed, not one had all the required permits – not surprising, since getting them was a huge bureaucratic hassle. Sadly, the result is that all that an official has to do is to walk into a shop and demand to see their permits, threatening them with prosecution when, inevitably, they cannot produce them. So cash changes hands and the official moves on to the next victim.

Corruption in the UK is subtler, but driven by the same complexity – nowhere more so than in the planning system, which is highly complex and where outcomes hinge on the personal judgement of politicians and officials. Want to build a new retail complex? Fine, but the town could *really* use a new swimming pool (which might help us get re-elected), so if you would like to contribute to that, it would really help your application... Such things are quite routine, but utterly corrupt.

Rent seeking

Representative democracy is not designed to benefit vested interests groups, or establishment politicians and bureaucrats, but it does. And as well as corrupting people in the public sector, it corrupts the private sector too. For the more that the state grows, the more decisions are made politically, and the more money that legislators and officials control, the richer are the potential pickings for what economists call 'rent seeking' by businesses and others. (In this case, 'rent' means extracting a profit without a lot of effort.)

If you can throw some money at the political system to get a law changed in your favour, or a new regulation to keep out competitors, then you are in clover. It is brazen self-interest, but you can dress it up by talking about 'protecting the public from cowboy operators' and suchlike. Businesspeople are all in favour of free markets, except in their own sector, where they prefer to prey on political power to "widen the market and to narrow the competition," as Adam Smith put it in *The Wealth Of Nations* (1776). "The proposal of any new law or regulation," he continued, "ought never to be adopted till after having been long and carefully examined, not only with the most scrupulous, but with the most suspicious attention." Quite so.

Still, you can't blame businesspeople and other interest groups for giving it a shot. It is our managerialist, majoritarian democracy that gives them access to money and favours. What we should condemn is politicians' willingness to let state power support private interests. Any remotely streetwise person will realise that.

5 The momentum of ruthlessness

Thoughts on the causes of the present discontents

The 2008-9 financial crisis turned a long boom into a frightening bust. But it was not just an economic shock: it was shock to the West's political systems too. Folk had got used to economic growth and rising wages, so they saw no reason to cause political upsets. But then banks crashed, wages fell and people's savings shrank. Socialist ideologues gleefully assured us that this was the final crisis of capitalism, as foretold by Karl Marx . There was a sudden loss of faith in the economic system.

Politicians, central bankers and regulators were quick to blame corporate greed — which conveniently deflected attention from the role that their own spendthrift, over-exuberant, let-the-good-times-roll policies had in destabilising the financial system. They assured us they were on our side: they would bring irresponsible bankers to heel with tougher regulation, bonus caps and stress tests. And yet, and yet.... It had all happened on their watch: they had neither anticipated nor prevented the crisis; they were bailing out the banks with taxpayers' money; and their other policy, quantitative easing, seemed to restore the fortunes of those with financial assets rather better than those of ordinary people. It all fostered a growing public mood that nobody in authority could be trusted.

Populists and nationalists preyed on this discontent. Times are hard, so why are we allowing foreigners to take our jobs? Why are immigrants entitled to the housing, education and healthcare that we have paid for? Why do we let other countries export their goods to us instead of making things ourselves? Socialist ideologues got a boost too. We should tax the rich, they said, in order to compensate the many who have lost income through the greed of the few. We should have tougher management of the economy. Banks and industries should be nationalised and run for the people, not for profit. Capital should be brought under government control.

It was an alluring narrative. It seemed that things could not be worse, so what was to be lost by trying something completely new? And the fact that so few people now remember the Cold War, the Berlin Wall, the Iron Curtain and the horrors of communism and fascism clinched the argument. Nationalist and socialist politicians held no terrors for two-fifths of voters, and as a result they did surprisingly well in the polls.

To the loser, the spoils

Indeed, from the self-confidence within Team Corbyn, and the media frenzy over their performance, you would think that they had actually won the 2017 general election. In fact, they were 98 seats behind. Only the combination of other Left-wing parties, such as the Liberal Democrats and Scottish Nationalists, forced Conservative leader Theresa May to struggle to build a coalition.

It became accepted wisdom that those same young people, unafraid of socialism and rather attracted by the Corbynist vision, had broken their traditional habits and actually got out of bed in order to vote in droves for the new radicalism. People talked of a 'youthquake': Oxford Dictionaries even made it their Word of the Year. Only much later did we discover that there was no reality behind the word. In January 2018, the British Election Study revealed that young people had delivered far more tweets than votes: turnout among young people had not increased, and the 2017 turnout by under-21s had actually fallen compared to 2015.

It shows how streetwise and suspicious you need to be when there is spin about. Team Corbyn calculated that young people were more likely to be excited (and less likely to be scared) by radical socialism, so upping their turnout could make a big difference. And having lots of young, twittering supporters would make Old Labour ideas look modern and visionary. So they talked up the 'youthquake' idea, and even got the media, who rub shoulders with spin-doctors every day, to believe it. Which they were inclined to do anyway: for young people on the march boosts ratings, while young people not bothering to vote is hardly news.

Yet the idea persists that a radical socialist government is both achievable and close. Perhaps that is no surprise, given how fed up people are with managerialism in general and Conservative dithering and incompetence in particular. Love radical socialism or loathe it, there is no doubting that the managerialists' armour has worn thin. The evidence is all around: the ease with which socialist radicals overwhelmed the Labour moderates, the shock of the 2017 general election, and the 2018 local council elections in England, in which none of the main parties did well.

The rise of the radicals

In early 2018, I was arguing that we were past Peak Corbyn. Unfortunately I did not realise that we were nowhere near past Peak Tory Meltdown. So it is clear that Corbyn's radical socialist vision still remains a big threat to the free society and free economy in the UK. British politics have become fractured to the point that anything could happen. Moreover, the man has shown himself fully able to climb peaks that nobody thought him capable of — like winning the Labour leadership. Even more resilient is the organisation behind him. Not the Labour Party — its MPs grit their teeth in embarrassment each time their Front Benchers rise to speak. What actually propels the radical socialist agenda are the grassroots networks that loosely make up what is called Momentum.

It is a brilliant name for a political movement. It implies no particular policies, but weight, importance and unstoppability. It is also more user-friendly than its previous incarnation, Militant, which suggested a bellicose extremism. That idea was not misplaced. The Militant 'tendency' was widespread in the 1980s. Using entryist tactics, and with the slogan "Better to break the law than break the poor," this Trotskyist group famously took control of Labour's operations in Liverpool. In London, meanwhile, Ken Livingstone (ably assisted by the current Shadow Chancellor John McDonnell) turned the Greater London Council into a stronghold of the so-called 'Loony Left' until an exasperated Conservative Prime Minister, Margaret Thatcher, finally abolished it.

She was not the only person to be alarmed at the rise of the extremists. So were the Labour Party themselves at the time. Remember the famous spat between the moderate Labour leader Neil Kinnock and Militant activist Derek Hatton, Deputy Leader of Liverpool City Council? Even Kinnock's predecessor, the staunchly Left-wing Michael Foot, launched an inquiry into Militant, which found that its policies and operations were incompatible with the Labour Party, and recommended expelling it. Jeremy Corbyn opposed the expulsions and led a 'Defeat the Witch-Hunt Campaign' against them. (Six years later, in 1988, he cosponsored a House of Commons resolution calling on the Soviet Union to rehabilitate Trotsky, which may say even more about his political sympathies — and priorities.)

Eventually, Militant changed its name to Militant Labour and came into the Party, just as Momentum today demands that its 40,000 (official) members should also be Labour Party members. But that does not limit its army of unofficial supporters, nor the entryism of its official ones — entryism made cheap and easy thanks to Ed Miliband's disastrous 2014 decision to open up leadership elections to anyone paying just £3 to join the Party. So now, moderate Labour MPs and councillors accuse Momentum of determined efforts to get them deselected as candidates, and complain that the Party leadership do little to prevent it. But given that several pro-Momentum candidates now sit on the Party's National Executive Committee, they can hardly expect it to.

Other moderates, including the former Leader of Haringey, Claire Kober, have spoken of threats and intimidation, while MP Stella Creasy said she had similarly been targeted by Left-wing thugs. In the 2015 and 2017 general elections there were widespread complaints of 'mob-Mentum' bullying and intimidation of candidates and party workers on all sides — though Momentum denies any of its official members were involved. Still, it is a worrying new trend in UK politics: intimidation has become as central to UK elections as rosettes and leaflets once were. The Committee on Standards in Public Life reported that 68% of Conservative Candidates in the 2017 election were victims of social media abuse, including threats of violence, sexual assault and damage to property. Then so were 36% of Labour candidates (on which wing of the Party, I wonder?). But candidates in closely fought seats will tell you that the intimidation was by no means only online.

Apologists for terror

It sounds like an exaggeration to call any of the leadership of the Labour Party in Parliament 'Trotskyist' or 'Marxist' or even 'Communist'. And yet, 200 years and 100+ million deaths later, the radicalism that Karl Marx inspired still has a powerful influence over the Left in the UK. Shadow Chancellor John McDonnell, at a SOAS (naturally) event in London on the bicentenary of Marx's birth, stated plainly that Marxism was one of the biggest influences on Corbyn's Labour Party, before going on to revive Marx's idea that capitalism was 'crisis-ridden' and claim that people were flocking to Marxist ideology as an escape from conventional politics. Nor did he say it with regret. In a 2006 interview with the (Trotskyist) Alliance for Workers' Liberty, he named the most significant influences on his thought as "the fundamental Marxist writers of Marx, Lenin and Trotsky." In a 2013 speech he said "Look, I'm straight, I'm honest with people: I'm a Marxist." And when the BBC political pundit Andrew Marr asked him if he really was, he did not exactly deny it.

Only crackpots, or academics cocooned in our state-run universities, could really endorse Marxism today. It would mean believing in the coming revolution and dictatorship of a suddenly self-aware proletariat, followed by the withering away of the state as a truly classless era dawns. But time has moved on, and in reality, capitalism and the state have proved far more robust. The peasant revolution never happened. Capitalism enriched the masses. With wealth came education and a different sort of self-awareness. People came to value capitalism and its products more, not less, and people became more socially mobile. The theory of Marx's *Das Kapital* seems no closer to modern reality than the rantings of Hitler's *Mein Kampf*.

Though Hitler was responsible for only a sixth of the slaughter done in Marx's name, in other respects their legacy is similar. Both

47

had the street thugs, the informers, the secret police, the labour camps, the torturers, and the death squads: they had to have them, simply to stay in control. The fact that anyone can claim allegiance to either ideology (or even equivocate about them) is shocking. Yet while Nazism is reviled, socialism is indulged, even celebrated, as a vision that can sweep away today's cronyism and put the people in charge. To the streetwise, and the living victims of socialist cronyism, such doublethink is terrifying.

It is also terrifying that socialists take no responsibility at all for the atrocities committed on their watch. As a supporter of capitalism, I am willing to accept that South Korea, with all its cronyism, protectionism and interventionism, is a working product of beliefs like mine. Even with those imperfections, its people are largely free and in just 65 years have risen out of poverty and wartime devastation to number among the world's richest. I would also not mind being associated with Hong Kong, Singapore, and many others, despite their obvious faults. But no socialist will accept North Korea today, or the Soviet Union, or Mao's China in the recent past, as practical examples of their own ideology. They insist that those are or were not 'real' socialism, but a 'perverted' version of it. Venezuela? "It went wrong," John McDonnell told the BBC's *Sunday Politics* in May 2018. "I do not think it was a socialist country.... I do not think they've been following the socialist policies that Chávez was developing." (Hugo Chávez being the former President, whose rule over this oil-rich state was marked by chronic shortages and currency crises.) Well, what passes for capitalism round the planet today is only a perverted version of that too, but at least it didn't kill 100 million people, terrorise more and impoverish the rest. It is shocking that prominent and intelligent people can still maintain the fantasy that it is possible to impose a collectivist ideology without the brutal coercion that Marx in *The Communist Manifesto* called "revolutionary terror". Sadly, that *is* real socialism.

Theory and reality

You must also be streetwise to the Left's tendency to compare their theory with others' reality. Capitalism is obviously flawed, they argue: just look at all the cronyism, monopoly and sharp practice. That is why we need socialism, a beautiful system based on the sublime virtues of altruism, fraternity and cooperation. But when you point out the awful reality of socialist regimes, you are told that each one was actually a perversion of a beautiful, sublime, virtuous, altruistic, fraternal and cooperative ideal. So you can't count the purges and famines under Lenin and Stalin in Russia, Mao in China, Pol Pot in Cambodia, the Kims in North Korea and others in Ethiopia, Vietnam or Somalia against socialism. Nor the slaughtering insurgencies in Angola, Peru, Laos, Albania and countless others. Nor the recent turmoil in Zimbabwe or Venezuela. But socialists can count cronyism, monopoly and sharp practice against capitalism.

As a supporter of capitalism, I am happy to compare the reality of capitalism with the reality of socialism because I think it is a first-round knockout. I am also happy to compare the ideal of capitalism with the ideal of socialism, because I think it is a second-round knockout. But you can't hail a victory for either system by pitting its ideal theory against the other's practical reality.

As for that reality, just as Prohibition inevitably produced gangsters like Al Capone, Bugs Moran and Machine-Gun Kelly, so socialism inevitably produced gangsters like Stalin, Mao and Mugabe. Socialism cannot succeed without state power and the ability to stop individuals deviating from the collective programme. And the people who are most effective at that are the more ruthless ones; so they are the ones that get to the top. Jeremy Corbyn might be a very nice person who loves children and pussycats. But it is street thugs who got him where he is — and who will eventually usurp him.

The wealth-killing agenda

And what of their agenda? Political rights do not mean much for long when extremists get into office. People who are certain they know what is right cannot allow elections or referenda or legislatures to stand in the way of that. Civil rights and liberties have never lasted long under regimes that set the collective purpose and cannot live with dissent.

Property rights too. Private property too is seen as something that exists for those in power to seize or control for the benefit of the collective. Indeed, this has become a common presumption, thanks to the managerialists, who also seek licence to take people's money for their chosen public purposes, and the power to take property for use in public projects. So the principle that your property should be secure from seizure by the authorities has already been broken: we are just talking about a matter of degree.

Unfortunately, countries do not prosper without property rights. A solid respect for private property is the main institution determining wealth creation and economic growth. Research by the Property Rights Alliance shows that other factors—civil liberties, political rights and press freedom—are also important, but a long way behind property rights in the growth stakes. And the things that kill economic growth are corruption, regulation, inflation and trade barriers—all of which the Momentum agenda would increase.

The radical Left's talk is all about inequality (more on that myth later) and that 'the rich' should pay more to support public services such as health and education. But top earners already pay half the nation's income tax and the biggest slice of most others. And remember, the majority of people in the *Sunday Times Rich List* are self-made businesspeople who have created wealth (and jobs, and goods that people value) rather than inherited it. When the Corbynist Shadow Minister Jon Trickett vowed to bring the richest Brits to a "shuddering halt", it would, unfortunately, be halting the very drivers of progress. We are already past the peak of the Laffer Curve, which plots tax rates against revenues. Further tax hikes will yield the government less money, not more, and would drive creative talent abroad—as it did in the 1970s, when top income tax rates reached 83% (with a 15% add-on for investment income).

Propping up or reinventing failure

And what of the policies for sweeping nationalisation of utilities, transport and human services? Sadly, the streetwise economist has more than enough evidence that throwing other people's money at nationalised state monopolies will not change or improve them.

Despite Gordon Brown's huge increase in the education budget, including an ambitious programme of constructing new school buildings (on credit, and whether the local community wanted them or not), parents who do have the choice to send their children to independently managed but state-funded 'Free Schools' queue up to do so. Their experience is not unique: the rise of Charter Schools in the US, and the abundance of low-cost private schools in China and India, show how fed up parents everywhere are with state schooling.

As for state welfare, how can we justify spending more on it when the UK is already one of the richest countries in the world? State welfare is an abject, over-bureaucratic, over-centralised failure. Welfare and pensions are the biggest item on the government's budget: if they are not getting people out of poverty, we need to do something else, not simply resort to more centralisation or spending yet more taxpayers' money.

The NHS is a classic example of how and why our managerialist authorities prop up socialist failure. As one of Tony Blair's health ministers, Lord Norman Warner, told the Adam Smith Institute in June 2018, "Throwing money at an unreformed NHS is pointless. We threw money at in the Blair years [when the budget rose by a third], and they didn't know how to spend it." You can't improve the performance of a rusty 1948 engine by putting more fuel into it. Because the health and social services bureaucracies do not mesh together, for example, nearly two million NHS England beds (i.e. about 4% of them) were occupied by each patient a day or more longer than necessary. Since hospitals consume two-thirds of NHS spending, that alone wastes nearly about 2.7% of the budget, about £3 billion. But that is only one example of general and chronic inefficiency — which is exactly what a streetwise economist expects to see in any monopoly where there are scant competitive pressures to be efficient because most customers have no real option of choosing another provider. So despite the vast budget, the NHS monopoly is poor at delivering even its most important functions: outcomes for some life-critical conditions such as stroke are no better than those in the Czech Republic.

Streetwise economists are not only aware that monopolies, public or private, have little incentive to deliver customers a good and efficient service. They also know that when the customers are not even paying, but someone else is – in this case, UK taxpayers – then the focus on customer service evaporates. Certainly, most of us want to make sure that everyone has access to decent healthcare, however rich or poor they might be. But most other countries – including many close to home such as France and the Netherlands – manage to combine that objective with greater customer sovereignty and (therefore) greater efficiency and cost-effectiveness, not to mention public satisfaction. Yet it is difficult to take the NHS in this direction, not because of any economic problem, but because of a seemingly impassable political one.

Clement Atlee's 1945 government nationalised coal, rail and steel, and created new state health, education and welfare systems. While the industries have been privatised, welfare has been greatly simplified, and education is at last starting to be opened up, patchily, to some parental choice, the NHS remains at its core a centralised state-run monopoly. So it is the last redoubt of those who believe passionately in the merits of nationalised state industries and services, and there is no limit to the efforts that some will expend to defend it. Whatever its reality, the *theory* of state healthcare must be protected. As we have seen, when politicians are confronted by a powerful and passionate lobby group, they very commonly give into it, and that is what has happened in health policy in the UK. It is certainly possible to design a healthcare system that is financed by customers and driven by their choices, and where the state ensures that everyone has access. But you will almost never hear that vision articulated by politicians of any party. Rather than face the Left's wrath, and have to worry that public concern will be stirred up by a 'project fear' campaign, they slip into managerialist mode and reassure everyone that they will preserve the system, often centralising it yet further and drawing its focus even further away from customers by expanding the state-controlled funding even more. On this front, therefore, the Cor-Mentum agenda is already, and firmly, in place.

And then there are the plans to renationalise industries such as rail, water, electricity and gas. If the current owners were to be compensated, the cost for taxpayers would run into billions. If they were not—and their property was simply seized—that would save a shock wave through the financial markets. No streetwise investor would touch the UK for years. Sure, the privatised industries are not perfect. There is too little competition in them. But at least you now get some choice (years ago, the nationalised telephone system's idea of competition was that you could have either a black handset, or a gray one). Taxpayers are better off too: nearly all the old nationalised industries made losses. But a streetwise economist doesn't believe any claims that state monopolies can be made entrepreneurial and dynamic. A monopoly is never entrepreneurial and dynamic, because it doesn't have to be: customers have no alternative. A state monopoly is even worse, because it can hold taxpayers to ransom.

Our capital-hating democracy

John McDonnell said that as Chancellor, he would bring in capital controls. He would have to, because money would quickly flood out of the country. Years ago I asked City of London friend: if the City decided to move all its clients' capital out of the country, how long would that take? He deliberated for some moments, then answered: "About fifteen minutes." Today it would be more like fifteen seconds. McDonnell would not even have got his pen out to sign the order.

Imprisoning investors in a capital-hating country would be an astonishing assault on individuals' property, even though we have seen it before. The old blue UK passports had a page at the back, headed 'Exchange Control Act 1947'. During the Wilson-Callaghan years, you had to list all your foreign currency transactions there. (That seems bizarre today, when you can buy as much foreign currency as you like, round the clock and almost anywhere.) Even more bizarre, you could not take more than £50 out of the country: a fair bit of money back then, but still not enough to pay for a week's family holiday. Travellers would stuff illicit £50 notes down their socks: such controls turn ordinary people into criminals.

What the capital-controlling managerialists of the Left forget is that free and healthy capital markets are essential for economic growth, because (as the International Monetary Fund will tell you) investment is what fuels growth. You invest so that you can produce things better and quicker: to make better use of your (and everyone's) time and effort. But the managerialists see taxes on capital funds as a nice little earner (and regulate the socks off them too). Then everyone wonders why people are not saving and investing, and why our productivity is so low. The streetwise economist knows darn well why.

Eliminating the competition

The Cor-Mentum answer is that the UK is under-investing because 'the rich' prefer to hide their cash in places with low capital taxes (such as the Isle of Man, Jersey, Cayman or the Bahamas) rather than patriotically investing it in the UK. Their solution is to close down these 'tax havens' down. And managerialists of Left and Right happily agree. After all, they would have no Budget problems if they could just bump taxes up and up without taxpayers having anywhere else to escape to. So they smear low-capital-tax jurisdictions as places where the rich can avoid paying their share for public services, sip cocktails on yachts, and launder their dirty money.

It is just guff, designed to stir up public prejudice. Today, low-tax areas have some of the toughest financial rules in the world, and follow the international agreements on money laundering. Indeed, they are more transparent and diligent about it than the UK or US, precisely because it is their livelihood: these places mostly have little else going for them. And while they have low taxes on capital, they are not exactly tax 'havens'. In the Cayman Islands, for example, taxes account for 38% of GDP—about the same as the UK. They just levy their taxes on consumption rather than capital. As a result, more investment money comes into them than into countries with high capital taxes, like the UK. All of which shows that the best way to boost investment and growth is not to close them down, but to follow their example.

Remember also that most people with money to invest are not cocktail-sipping billionaires. They are ordinary people with pensions savings. Places like Jersey collect all that money, make sure it is not all taxed away, and then send this valuable pool of investment capital out to places where it creates jobs and economic growth. It might go to the UK and US, but it also goes to Latin America, Africa, the Far East and other places where growth and prosperity are sorely needed. The 'tax havens' are not so much playgrounds for the rich as drivers of the spectacular rise in world living standards over the last thirty years. The only people who would benefit from their demise are high-spending politicians. As streetwise savers know.

Should we be worried about tax avoidance anyway? Yes, but not for the reasons that John McDonnell and his colleagues would argue. His view is that if 'the rich' paid their full share of taxes, policies like nationalising the railways and sinking more money into the NHS would be easily affordable. So he would get tough on tax avoidance and evasion. (Notice how the two words are always conflated, even though they are completely different concepts. Evasion is where you do not fully disclose your liability to tax. That is a criminal offence. Avoidance is where you stay within the law, but navigate through the rules in order not to pay more tax than you really need to. That is common sense. Again, it is not just 'the rich' who do this: almost everyone who can, does — putting their savings into offshore funds, saving into pensions, even setting up companies to provide services to clients, rather than going on salary.) What should concern us is the fact that our tax rates are so high that it is worth people doing all this to avoid them; and that our tax rules are so complex that they become capable of exploiting.

If taxes were lower and simpler, people would willingly pay them. Indeed, after every episode, both in the US and UK, where the high taxes on the highest earners were cut, those same high earners actually contributed *more* tax revenue, not less. That was true of the Coolidge cut in the 1920s, the Kennedy cut in the 1960s, the Reagan cut in the 1980s and the Bush cut after that; it was true also of the Howe-Lawson cuts in the UK. Quite simply, if taxes are too high, it becomes worth people's while to avoid them. And there is another point that should deter those who think that clamping down on avoidance will unleash a wall of money for state projects. A large part of the supposed 'avoidance gap' in tax receipts exists only because it costs the Treasury more to pursue people for questionable avoidance tactics than it actually raises in doing so. So you cannot hope to raise revenues just by 'getting tough' because 'getting tough' is itself expensive. As any streetwise economist is aware.

Denigrating economic freedom

In *Who's Who*, the Shadow Chancellor John McDonnell lists among his hobbies "generally fermenting [*sic*.] the overthrow of capitalism." It is an ambition he confirmed to the BBC's *Sunday Politics* in May 2018. "I want a socialist society," he said. "And that means transforming [the economy] in a way that radically changes the system as it now is."

Really? Unfortunately for its critics, capitalism actually produces the goods, which is more than socialism does. In its early days, folk like Karl Marx argued that socialism, being more 'scientific' and 'rational' than 'anarchic' markets, would outpace capitalism. It didn't. Its first test-bed, the USSR, lagged far behind the capitalist US. By 1976 there were about 100m cars in the US; in the USSR there were just 5m, with waiting lists as long as ten years. By 1976, two-thirds of Soviet citizens had a refrigerator, something the US achieved in the 1930s. (They had to wait two years, then got a postcard giving them a one-hour slot to pick it up, or lose it.) Soviet citizens consumed half as much fish and meat (which was also of lower quality) and six times less fruit and vegetables, but twice the quantity of potatoes, as their US counterparts. Nor did the Soviets even achieve equality: after the 1970s the poorer sections of society endured rapidly declining meat consumption. Yet the Soviet Union wasted more food than the US: less than two-thirds of its milk production (the world's biggest) actually made it into people's kitchens, and 15% of meat and 40% of fruit and vegetables were spoiled during production or storage.

On the US measure of poverty, half the Soviet population were poor. Around a quarter could not afford a winter coat. The USSR had the world's highest doctor-patient ratio, but many of those doctors could not perform basic tasks. While life expectancy shot up in the West, it actually fell in the USSR in the 1970s. There were thirty times more typhoid cases and twenty times more measles cases than in the US. Infant mortality in Russia has lagged the West for decades.

That reality was obvious even before the Berlin Wall came down and made it glaringly so. Leftist intellectuals therefore had to come up with another line. The trouble with capitalism, they suggested, was not that it would produce *less* than socialism. The trouble was that it produced *too much*. Capitalist 'consumerism' was excessive and wasteful.

It is easy to say that if you are on a good state salary with generous pension and fringe benefits. But it is an insult to the millions of ordinary individuals who actually need those cars, fridges, meat, fruit and medical services. It is an even bigger insult to the billions languishing on dollar-a-day poverty in socialist countries. But then it is a curious fact that, for all their emphasis on 'the people', socialists do not actually trust people to do the right things, and instead make the decisions for them. And it is surprising how so many of their policies actually end up robbing the poorest people, rather than helping them. Well, perhaps not so surprising, to the streetwise economist.

6 What is seen and what is not seen

The big defect in most economic and social policy today is that it focuses on the obvious, without thinking through how things actually work. To many, it seems obvious that we can help the poor by taking money from the rich, or that we can boost domestic investment by preventing capital from going abroad. But in fact such policies create additional, deeper and more general problems – such as discouraging enterprise or shattering people's confidence that their property is secure – which makes them counterproductive.

The French politician and writer Frédéric Bastiat (1801-1850) explained this defect in his story *That Which Is Seen And That Which Is Not Seen*. If a careless boy breaks a shop window, he wrote, it creates six francs' worth of work for the glazier – who now has six francs more to spend in the local economy, boosting other local businesses too. What is *seen*, a business boom, looks great. But what is *not seen* is the fact that the shopkeeper now has six francs *less* to spend on other things – completely negating any gain. If the *seen* consequences were all there were to it, then the government might as well employ squads to go out and smash windows as a way of boosting economic growth. That is plainly daft: but, dominated by the *seen*, it is exactly how managerialist policy is made.

The error of wage and price controls

Take minimum wages and the National Living Wage. They are promoted as a way of helping the poor by making sure that all workers are paid enough to live on. They raise wages: that is *seen*. But they do not help the poorest because the very poorest are not in work at all. And the vast majority of people on minimum wages are not even in poor households: many are students, or retired people just keeping active, or partners of middle and high earners who want to bring in some pin money. If you really wanted to help the poor, you would be better to use the Working Tax Credit, which encourages poorer people into work (since a paying job is the best welfare programme there is), or easing employment regulation so as to encourage small businesses (in particular) to hire people.

But the effect of minimum wage legislation is to deny people jobs. As the US President Jimmy Carter's peanut-grower brother, once put it, "Hell, some people ain't worth the minimum wage." In his bluff way, he was just saying what every streetwise economist knows: unless workers can generate more value for a business than all the costs of employing them (wages, national insurance, pensions, management time), then there is no point in taking them on in the first place. Minimum wages make getting a job harder for exactly the sorts of people we most want to help: people who are less valuable to employers such as those with few skills, young people starting out, immigrants with poor English, and so on. So the real effect of the policy is to trap people on state welfare. Why do you now order your McDonalds hamburger from a touch screen? Easy: machines are much cheaper than workers on the National Living Wage.

Price controls, such as energy price caps and rent controls, have unintended and damaging consequences too. When legislation limits prices, suppliers find it less profitable to sell their product. So they produce less, or stop producing it completely, or switch to other lines where the prices are not regulated. If bakers are unable to charge the market price for a basic bread loaf, for example, they might simply take loaves off the shelves, leaving none for customers to buy, or may bake more cakes and specialist breads, which customers will find more expensive. On the other side of the counter, consumers will see that bread prices are being kept low, and will demand more bread — even more than they can eat, if they can get it. You may think that an exaggeration, because there is only so much bread that anyone can consume. But you would be wrong. If a product is artificially cheap, people will waste it. Or they will use it for other purposes: when bread prices were fixed below the market price in the 1960s, bread became an economic way to fill gaps in brick and plaster work, and ingenious builders cleared the shelves.

The result of price-fixing, therefore, is more demand and less supply, with prices not being allowed to bring things into balance. Rent control is a particularly shocking example. Again, the *seen* is that caps on rent rises make accommodation cheaper for everyone. The *unseen* reality is quite different. For a start, the policy requires a whole industry of rent tribunals and valuations and enforcement. But more fundamentally, if landlords cannot cover their costs, they will maintain their property less well or take it off the market entirely. The result is that people struggle to find rented homes, flats are gone within minutes of being advertised, and buildings are poorly maintained. Rent control is why much of New York's rented accommodation has peeling paint, mouldy carpets, damp walls and rotting woodwork, and why prospective tenants in rent-controlled Stockholm languish an average of fifteen years on waiting lists. Unless you have connections with property owners or local government insiders, you could be completely out of luck.

Politicians might crow about their success in keeping living costs down through such controls. But who is really helped by a regulation that makes things cheap, but unobtainable? If people cannot afford essentials, the better policy is to help them get a job, or give them cash so that they can. Yet the managerialists continue to impose, or propose, these and countless other price caps — on electricity and gas prices, phone packages, payday loans, rail fares, college tuition fees and more. The *seen* policies are popular; the *unseen* effects are baleful. They have always been baleful, even since Hammurabi of Babylon came up with the idea forty centuries ago.

Environmental misdiagnoses

Environmental policy is another area where the *seen* eclipses the *unseen*, and policy is based on the former. Take the entirely plausible worry that industry is using up the world's resources. The streetwise economist knows that capitalism does not just *use* resources; it *creates* them. Tungsten was merely a contaminant hated by tin miners for centuries until we found its value in strengthening metals. And whatever you think of fossil fuels, deserts were worthless until we found commercial applications for the oil and gas beneath them. Even rocks are becoming valuable resources thanks to fracking. Precisely because oil is valuable to us, we have explored for it and found more of it than we've ever known before.

The fear that we are running out of resources is what the economist Tim Worstall calls the 'No Breakfast Fallacy'. Do you look in the 'fridge, see that you only have eggs and bacon enough for one day, then despair that you will have no breakfast the next? No, you go down to the supermarket and stock up with more. The fact that we know only of ten years' reserves of some key mineral does not mean that only ten years' supply exists, after which we're doomed. We have only ten years' known reserves because it is not worth the effort of exploring for more until we're running short—just as it is not worth cramming the fridge with a month's worth of provisions. When it becomes profitable to look for more, we simply start digging the other side of the mountain.

Activists tell us to buy local, to reduce 'food miles'. But as long ago as 2008, Christopher Weber and Scott Matthews showed that four-fifths (83%) of the greenhouse gas emissions associated with food come from the production phase: transport is only a tenth (11%) and final delivery to retailers is less than a twentieth (4%). That is because food is transported efficiently, in bulk. The majority of 'food miles' are those you make bringing it home from the shop. Even then, foreign produce can save energy. Spain's sunshine produces tomatoes that in Britain require heated greenhouses.

Almost everything said and done about 'saving the planet' is wrong, or creates other undesirable consequences (Rentokil, for example, reported a 60% increase in house moth infestations over the four years to 2018, because our eco-friendly washing machines do not kill moth larvae at 30°C.). From the talk, you might think that we are getting more polluted by the hour. But a century ago, our streets were covered with rotting horse dung. Two-thirds of a century ago, the London smog killed 12,000 people. Half a century ago, most city buildings were black from coal and diesel fumes. The reality is that the world is getting cleaner—because we are getting richer, and richer people demand a cleaner environment. The economist Steven Pinker discovered that when poor countries develop they initially get dirtier. But there is a turning point. As they get richer still, they start getting cleaner. Quite simply, once people have secured their basic needs, like food and clean water, they start wanting luxuries like education, healthcare and a clean environment. The streetwise way to improve the environment is not to kill off capitalism, but to embrace it.

Mistakes about inequality

Yet another debate where the popularity of the *seen* leads economists and politicians into destructive policy is inequality. We are told that the divide between rich and poor is widening, so politicians should intervene, curb the excesses and help the worst off. The trouble is that the Cor-Mentum idea of bringing wealth-creators to a 'shuddering halt' would not help anyone. If people have no prospect of making themselves wealthy from the process, why should they bother to develop the life-improving products that others willingly pay for?

But even the *seen* statistics on inequality conceal the *unseen* reality. During the recession of the late 2000s, everyone became worse off. But wealthier people became even worse off than the average. So according to the statistics, inequality fell. Obviously we do not want to reduce inequality by making everyone worse off: but that would be the effect of many of the policies advocated.

Or again: Oxfam's annual report on world inequality suggests that a handful of people control half the world's wealth. But then on their figures, the poorest people on the planet, with 'negative' wealth, are Harvard graduates. Hardly: they may have a $200,000 student debt and no assets, but their expected average salary of $90,000 will soon make them rich. So we should not base any policies on them. Nor should we care that Bill Gates is worth $92 billion. Wealth is not a fixed pie: wealth is something you grow. Bill Gates did it by creating technology that millions of people bought because it transformed their lives. That made him financially richer — but it made all those millions richer in different and even more important ways. Now the Gates Foundation gives more to people in developing countries in one year than Oxfam does in fifteen. And though again you would never believe this from the hype, global wealth inequality has actually *fallen* over the last few decades. That is because of countries like China, India and Vietnam embracing enterprise and free trade. Streetwise reformers do not care about the wealth of the rich: they care about the welfare of the poor. And every day for the past 25 years, around 138,000 people have lifted themselves out of dollar-a-day poverty, thanks to their countries opening up to world trade. In Vietnam, income has risen from $100 per head before its liberalising 1986 reforms to around $2000 per head today. Just a little dose of capitalism has made them twenty times better off. Only the places that have rejected markets and trade have bucked the trend. In Venezuela, socialism has condemned three-quarters of the population to poverty, with many lacking basic necessities like food and medicine, despite the country having the world's largest oil reserves.

Nor has wealth inequality risen in the UK, despite all the stories. Indeed, it fell massively during the century up to 1980, and has flat-lined since. And according to the Office for National Statistics, UK income inequality is now at its lowest level for thirty years. Moreover, when you look beyond raw incomes, and at what people actually have available to spend after they pay tax or receive state benefits, inequality is even less. The gross incomes of the top fifth are twelve times those of the bottom fifth: after tax and benefits, this falls to just four times. And remember, when people talk disparagingly of the wealth of the 'top one per cent', the global one per cent includes around five million UK citizens.

The executive pay non-problem

Yet what really annoys people is not inequality, but the unfairness of undeserved income. The soaring pay of FTSE 100 chief executives often cited as an example. But that is the *seen* again. The *unseen* is that good Chief Executive Officers are more important to their companies than ever. FTSE 100 firms are now larger and more international, and need exceptional people to run them. Investors know that a CEO makes a huge difference to a company's value: that is why share prices rise and fall as good CEOs come and go. When Burberry's CEO Angela Ahrendts announced her departure, it wiped £536m off the company's value. Likewise when Steve Ballmer resigned as Microsoft CEO, the firm's value jumped by £20bn. In any case, despite all the complaints about the 'one per cent', 100 chief executives out of a workforce of 32 million is not one per cent. It is about 0.0003%. Why should we give a fig about that?

And yet the High Pay Centre, a Leftist pressure group, campaigned successfully for new government rules to force FTSE 100 firms to publish the pay ratios between their CEOs and general workers, and to 'name and shame' those with the biggest divide. Such statistics are nonsense: a cleaning firm with many low-skilled workers will always look less equal than an IT firm with many high-skilled employees; Tesco will look less equal than Goldman Sachs, even if their CEOs are paid the same. Attacking the CEOs of our largest companies will merely make it harder for those firms to bring the best leadership to the UK, leading to declining productivity and job losses — which hardly helps ordinary workers.

Focus and policy

The Canadian activist Naomi Klein claims that inequality is psychologically damaging, shortens our lives, makes us less charitable, leads to higher murder rates, and spreads unhappiness. (All based on highly selective figures, as *The Economist* pointed out.) But streetwise experiments show that people are actually very bad at judging how equal or unequal their country is. Their answers are no better than random. Perhaps it is simply *talking* about inequality that makes people miserable — in which case we should shut up about it, and pursue wealth-creating policies rather than wealth-destroying ones.

If you really want to help the poorest, you should focus on that, rather than get distracted by the inequality myths. And probably the best policy, as Adam Smith knew, is to get tax and regulation out of their way. The economist Ryan Bourne points out that the poorest 20% of households in the UK spend around 60% of their income on essentials: housing, food, transport, clothing and utilities. So the taxes and excise duties on all those things are highly regressive. And government interventions raise their prices even further. Planning restrictions make housing unaffordable; protectionist trade barriers raise prices on food, footwear and clothing; while national and local transport policies stifle innovation. Scrapping all this spaghetti of controls and regressive taxes would help the poorest and boost economic growth — which would help them even more.

One of the most shameful taxes on the poor is the 'renewables levy' added to energy bills. It is the managerialist response to environmentalist campaigns, fuelled by commonsense-seeming sound bites, but actually ignoring the *unseen* reality. The first reality to notice is that because heating and lighting costs take up a larger proportion of the income of poorer households, they suffer far more than those who impose the policy on them. The second is that much of the money raised merely enriches landowners with estates on windy hills suitable for turbines. Some of it goes towards solar panels, which are highly ineffective in our cloudy country, generating less than a tenth of their potential output. For thirty weeks of the year they generate nothing; only on about eight days a year do they generate more than half of what they are capable of. The lifetime output of a 5MW solar park could be generated in just 36 hours by a nuclear power station taking up one fiftieth of the ground space. Even wind and solar combined would only generate more than 60% of their potential for a day and a half each year, and would be below 20% of capacity for over half the year. Poorer households might well wonder why money is being forced out of them for this. The answer is: to make their managerialist masters look virtuous.

Failed thinking on redistribution

Sadly, policies that might actually help the *poor* have been eclipsed by the idea of reducing *inequality*. But what does that mean? Are we talking about inequality of wealth or of income? If we equalise everyone but then some successful people go on to earn more from grateful customers, do we accept the resulting inequality? Or do we insist that everyone earns the same — in which case, what is to stop some people simply putting their feet up, because they will earn just as much as they do by working? Should we focus only on money, or compensate people for non-financial inequalities, such as the difficulty or danger unpleasantness of their job, or whether they live and work in a nice or less nice area? How do we assess that? And should we be aiming to apply redistribution to everyone in the world (which is hardly likely to be a popular idea with any Westerner, who would see their earnings or wealth slashed), or does it apply only to those in our own country (which leaves the bulk of the poverty problem untouched).

But then calls for redistribution to promote equality (or merely the more fluid idea of 'social justice') will never succeed because, however appealing is the broad concept, nobody actually agrees on the practical details. Exactly who should be taxed, and in what amounts? Who should get how much when the money is disbursed? What does 'social justice' suggest we should pay different groups — nurses, doctors, teachers, train drivers, civil servants, lecturers, bus drivers, architects, divers, electricity workers, car mechanics and others? Right now the labour market decides it, on the simple principle of supply and demand. But if officials had to decide everyone's pay on the basis of 'social justice' or people's 'value to society', nobody would accept the result: almost everyone would say they are worth more. That is hardly a recipe for 'social solidarity': it would be a war between each different group for a bigger share, just as it was in the fractious days of the 1960s and 1970s.

The redistribution approach also forgets that wealth does not just *exist*, to be shared out by the authorities. Wealth has to be *created*, and we should be building the conditions that allow people to create more of it, not doing things that discourage them by making wealth creation less worthwhile. The charlatan economist Thomas Piketty says that wealth owners get increasingly rich because of the return their capital generates: so we need 80% income taxes to rebalance the equation. But streetwise economists know that creating and keeping wealth, and generating continuing returns is not easy. It requires effort, vision, imagination, entrepreneurship, risk-taking, flair and even a bit of luck. Risks do not always pay off. Fortunes are lost through mistakes, mismanagement and misfortune. Competitors may poach your customers. Uncertainties like war, recession or changes in fashion can ruin you. New technology makes old capital goods worthless, as the owners of hot metal printing presses or machines that once made slide rules, typewriters or eight-track tape recorders discovered. Capital does not guarantee anyone lifetime riches: capital needs to be built up, maintained, refreshed, nurtured, and applied to create value in ways that are appropriate to the time and circumstances. Losing it is the easy part.

This makes it obvious that we can't make ourselves, and future generations, better off unless we create wealth and continue creating it. We need to foster the conditions that promote wealth creation, and ensure that wealth creators are adequately rewarded for the time, vision, risk-taking, money and effort they put into the process. Why should anyone do all that, and take all those risks, if high taxes leave them little or no better off than others who just take things easy? It is a big world, travel is easy, knowledge and skills have become more important than machines and factories, and as we saw in the Brain Drain of the 1970s (that time of 98% tax rates), people can easily up sticks and take their human capital with them. That is no way to promote equality and prosperity.

The gender non-gap

It is routinely asserted that there is a 'gender gap' between how men and women are paid for similar work. The BBC and others have been publicly humiliated by the (*seen*) disparities. But in *unseen* reality, there is no significant gender gap, and policies based on that idea are ill founded.

True, there is a gender pay gap between *older* workers. That is why the BBC gets into trouble. Its presenters enjoy astonishing job security: in current affairs, few are under 40; not many are under 50; and the millionaire *Today Programme* presenter John Humphreys has just clocked up three-quarters of a century. In the overall economy too, female workers over 40 are paid less, on average, than their male counterparts. But the *unseen* reason is that when those workers first joined the workforce twenty or more years ago, there was indeed discrimination, and large gender pay gaps were common. So when employees get roughly equal annual increases, those gaps persist. That is certainly is an unjust hangover.

But culture has changed. Those entering the workforce today are much more likely to be valued and rewarded on equal terms. For women in their 20s, the gender gap was already closing in the mid-2000s. For those in their 30s, it disappeared entirely. It has even halved for those in their 40s. Today, there is still a pay gap: but it is not a gender pay gap. It is a motherhood and caring gap, because women usually take the lead in raising children and looking after older or disabled relatives. As a result, more women prefer flexible or part time working, and take more take years off from paid work to accommodate their caring work. But part timers and those on flexible hours are generally worth less to employers: they absorb more management time and are not always there when you need them. So people who want flexible work (mostly women) may settle for lower pay, or may take lower-grade jobs where flexible hours cause managers fewer problems. And hence a pay gap opens up. Likewise, people who take years off to raise children or look after relatives (mostly women again) fall behind in the lifetime pay progression. Women's earnings, which rise along with men's in their early years, suffer a 'caring' dip in their 20s or early 30s. Female earnings then resume their rise, but by then the men's earnings are ahead, since people are rewarded, in part, according to the length of their employment. It is a natural phenomenon that policy seemingly can't dent: Sweden's parental leave policy, for instance, is the world's most generous, allowing 480 days of paid leave for either parent; but it makes only a tiny difference, around one percentage point, to the pay differences between men and women after the caring gap.

The real causes of the crash

Look beyond the *seen* of the financial crash and you realise that it was caused by politicians and regulators — not by bankers and capitalism.

Recall the times. Cheap Chinese imports were keeping prices down, so the Bank of England kept interest rates low, which helped Gordon Brown's government to borrow on a record scale. The low interest rates prompted people to take out mortgages and buy houses, pushing up prices. People felt richer, so ran up credit card debts too. Things boomed, champagne flowed, but it was a fake boom that could not last. Our regulators seemed intoxicated too.

While the Bank expressed concern that the huge mortgage lender Northern Rock was failing, Brown's Financial Services Authority did nothing. Northern Rock collapsed six months later, and the panic spread from bank to bank.

America's policy was worse still. In 1977, US President Jimmy Carter signed the 'anti-redlining' law, which stopped lenders denying mortgages to people in poor areas. The intention was noble, but it forced the banks to issue what we now know as 'sub-prime' mortgages to customers who could not easily repay them. By 1985 these bad loans had nearly bankrupted America's Savings and Loan institutions, so the government bailed them out and forced them to merge — unwittingly making them 'too big to fail'.

In 1987, the US stock market plummeted on fears that other lenders could collapse. Unrelated, Japan's banks failed. Mexico, Argentina and Russia defaulted on their government debts. But each time, the US and UK authorities responded by flooding the world with cash. After 9/11, the Federal Reserve took US interest rates down from 6.25% to just 1%. That boosted confidence, but (*seen* and *unseen* again) with loans now six times cheaper, mortgage applications soared. Lenders, high on the Fed's cash, happily issued more sub-prime loans. Indeed, Bill Clinton's 1991 strengthening of the anti-redlining law threatened them with stiff regulatory penalties if they didn't.

As more people bought houses, prices soared. Buying a house seemed a certain moneymaker, so more and more people did, whether or not they could afford it. The US mortgage institutions, Fannie Mae and Freddie Mac, went bust from bad loans. Banks borrowed thirty times their assets to finance yet more sub-prime mortgages. They knew they were overloaded with bad debt, so they sliced and diced it and sold it to London. No regulator raised a finger.

So the true culprits were not the customers who took out unaffordable loans, nor the bankers who obliged them — but the politicians and regulators who created a fantasy world that made it all seem sensible to them. But capitalism is resilient, and is still pulling millions out of poverty each year. What a crime it would be if, because we did not look beyond the *seen*, we regulated financial markets out of existence.

The unseen complexity of capital

Another thing that is *unseen* is that the value of capital, and its productive capacity to enrich everyone, depends not just on how much of it there is, but what it is, where it is, and how it all networks together.

Carmakers, for example, rely not just on their own production lines to make their product. They also rely on hundreds of parts suppliers who each employ specialist capital equipment of their own, and on distributors and dealers with showrooms and customer management systems. All this capital has to work together in order to create cars and get them to customers. If any part of the supply chain fails, all the other capital in the chain becomes useless, a wasted investment, until the link is restored.

To create the maximum output for the minimum cost and effort, capital goods of every kind — land, buildings, machines, supply chains, distribution systems and the rest — need to be integrated into their most productive uses. That is exactly what capital markets do: steering capital to its most productive niches in the productive network. Redistribution and nationalisation policies overlook how important, complex and delicate this network is. It has evolved over centuries, and continues to evolve as the realities of technology and demand change. You cannot just grab a bit of capital to use for other purposes and expect things to carry on. Like ripples on a lake, disruption will spread through the economy in ever-expanding circles. As things settle in a new arrangement, some enterprises and capital goods will lose their purpose and value — which means a real loss of the time, energy and effort invested in creating them.

Once again, the streetwise economist has to look behind the *seen*, and understand what is really going on *unseen*.

71

7 Robbing the poor

Over-simple explanations

Given the reality of Cor-Mentum ideas, why do they have so much power over the public debate? Perhaps because academics and commentators, having ivory-tower lives and educated and supported by the state, tend more to the Left. Yes, really: Left-liberals make up around 75% of UK academics, Conservatives only 12%. (Nor is that just down to brains: among the whole population, people in the top 5% of IQ break roughly equally between Left and Right.) And given this skew in our universities, which has widened since the 1960s, it is no wonder that campuses are so rife with Leftist groupthink — which might explain why almost all of them censor free speech on campus, and how our managerialist masters have become so infected with the same bug.

Another part of the reason is the *seen* versus the *unseen* again. It is easy to explain the merits of central 'planning' over market 'anarchy'. It is harder to appreciate that businesses do plenty of planning of their own, based on a much better understanding of customers' needs than any state planner could possibly possess. Likewise, it is easy to imagine the rational order that might be imposed on an economy. It is harder to grasp how, *unseen*, markets evolve and adapt, both rationally and efficiently, to the changing needs of society. Again, it is easy to argue that key services such as transport or utilities should be run in the public interest rather than for profit. It is harder to appreciate that competition is the best regulator, and that customers are better off in a competitive market where they can switch suppliers, rather than being trapped in a state monopoly. And it is easy to argue for greater equality. It is harder to explain the systematic harm that redistributionist policies do to incentives, morality and prosperity.

This gulf between simple, emotive but wrong explanations and complex, rational but more realistic ones explains why public policy so often produces the exact opposite of the intended outcomes. Focusing on the *seen* problems that can and do arise in commerce, and seeking to manage them, for example, our authorities load businesses with regulation after regulation. Large incumbent firms can deal with that: they are big enough to afford the necessary armies of compliance officers. But to small and new firms, the cost is disproportionate. (The huge cost of financial regulation, for example, explains why MetroBank was the first new high-street bank to get a banking licence in a century and a half.) The net result is that — *unseen* — innovation and competition are strangled.

The Cor-Mentum proposals to re-nationalise rail, utilities and other industries may seem the obvious solution to obvious problems. But the problems are misdiagnosed and the solution is wrong. One cause of rail's problems, for example, is that passengers have returned to rail travel in vast numbers since the operators were privatised; but the monopoly infrastructure quango, Railtrack, has not developed tracks and stations enough to cope. Another cause is that our supposedly 'privatised' rail industry is actually a series of regional monopoly operators, nominally private but in reality told what services to run (and how much profit they can make) by the state. In the few places where there is some competition, fares are significantly lower. For example, Virgin's fare on the West Coast route is 24% more than it charges on the East Coast route, where it faces competition. Between London and Crewe a peak train is £131 for a journey of 158 miles, while the 156 miles between London and Doncaster, where there is competition, costs £99. The two other competing operators are even cheaper, with Hull Trains charging £58 and with Grand Central charging £52. But such competition exists on just 1% of passenger miles travelled by rail.

Nationalisation would snuff out what little competition exists and turn the system into a single state monopoly. Sadly we have forgotten how bad that idea was. British Rail was characterised by falling passenger numbers, declining services and curly sandwiches. And because rail workers could hold the government to ransom, strikes and go-slows were chronic. Looking behind the *seen* to the *unseen*, a streetwise economist knows how poorly monopolies serve the public — particularly state monopolies.

The argument for intervention

The idea driving regulation is that markets sometimes fail: so government action is needed to correct this 'market failure'.

For example, it is said that markets cannot provide important 'public' goods like lighthouses, parks, roads or harbours, because nobody can charge customers for them and so make a profit. The reality, however, is that (particularly with modern IT to help us), many of these goods can be, and already are, provided very efficiently by markets, without the need to involve government. A second 'problem' is that sellers know a lot more about their products than customers (think used car dealers), which puts buyers at a disadvantage: so sellers must be licensed and regulated. But in reality, buyers are shrewder and better informed than the theorists imagine — particularly in an age of online reviews.

Another supposed 'failure' is that there are few suppliers in some markets, so government must intervene to curb monopolistic power. In reality, however, some markets (such as car making) have few sellers because the capital needed is great, which is a big barrier against others coming in, even though there is nothing else to prevent them. And economic experiments show that markets work amazingly well even when there are few players. Lastly, it is said that producers (such as factories) load costs on other people by polluting air and water or (like supermarkets) causing traffic congestion. But the only reason that producers can impose costs on others is because they are not charged for doing so: the solution is to employ markets *more*, not less.

And given what we know about government decision-making, it is clear that the bigger problem is not 'market failure' but government failure.

Government failure in the workplace

Even ignoring the politics and self-interest that shape government decisions, much intervention has the opposite effects of those intended. But every regulation is introduced for some reason, and even if the results are baleful, they each have their defenders, making them hard to remove. So they simply grow in number, making it hard for anyone even to know what the rules are, never mind follow them—particularly people trying to create and run new, innovative small businesses that might challenge the larger incumbents.

Employment law, for example, goes back to the Black Death, but was added to during the Industrial Revolution, then expanded fast in the 1960s and 1970s, with yet more added when Tony Blair signed the UK up to the EU Social Chapter. And more regulations have been added annually since. Employers now face an unfathomable clutter of minimum wage laws, working time and holiday pay regulations, laws to provide for flexible working and child care, rules on pensions contributions, rules on warnings and dismissals, the right to strike, recognition of trade unions, worker participation, and the 'TUPE' rules that protect workers' terms and conditions if a firm is taken over (lobbied for by trade unions as a perfect way to block privatisations and takeovers by more efficient managers and maintain their featherbedding at customers' expense).

Yet the streetwise reality is that all this legislation does not actually create and protect jobs. Indeed, it makes job creation harder, because it imposes huge time and money costs on UK businesses, particularly new, game-changing ones. It means that when firms hire someone, they take their life in their hands. If new employees do not work out, it is hard to remove them: fail to follow strict rules and procedures and you could end up in an Industrial Tribunal—costless for the worker, but cripplingly expensive for a small business. The result is that firms become more cautious about hiring in the first place, making it harder for people to find a job.

Those who are most disadvantaged by this are untried young people with few skills, and others who (say) may have weak English or be new to UK business culture, or for religious reasons will not work Saturdays or handle particular goods, making them less valuable to employers. They *could* make themselves more attractive by offering to take lower wages or fewer holidays, getting into work and demonstrating their potential to employers. But if employers are not allowed to pay below a national minimum, nor reduce time off, this happy option is not open. So they never get a foot on the jobs ladder and languish on welfare instead.

Rewarding the rich

The middle classes, however, are adept at milking the regulatory system. If anyone's proposals should be listened to with Adam Smith's "most suspicious attention," it is theirs.

Even today, countless business groups still convince our political leaders to give them near-monopolies. They call it 'regulating the market' and claim it is all for the public interest, but for them it has the happy effect of squeezing out the competition. It is why you need a licence to become anything from A to Z: acupuncturist, auctioneer, beauty therapist, boat hirer, childminder, doctor dog breeder, engineer, estate agent, farmer, hairdresser, lawyer, metal dealer, money lender, plant grower, property manager, publican, social carer, surveyor, taxi driver, teacher, window cleaner, or zookeeper.

We have known since Milton Friedman's 1939 study *Income From Independent Professional Practice* that professional licensing of doctors, lawyers, accountants and others brings benefits to those professions, but not the public. It does not protect customers from bad or incompetent service. It makes practitioners focus on getting paper qualifications, not developing practical skills. And anyway, who ever asks to see their accountant's or insurance agent's licence? Most people choose their professionals by reputation and word of mouth.

The *unseen* reality is that professional licensing allows practitioners to deliver a higher-cost service, a worse service, and less service (because their protected status gives them the time and money to play golf instead of working). Licensing also gives the established trade bodies enormous powers. The medical councils, for example, are really just professional trade unions with statutory powers, who can keep out new competitors and disqualify innovators simply because they disagree with their methods.

It is reminiscent of the mediaeval guilds. But at least in mediaeval times, people could move to the thriving 'liberties' on the outskirts of the city, where guild rules did not apply. That is why all the theatres that staged Shakespeare's plays, like the Rose and the Globe, were south of the Thames rather than in the City of London itself. These days, unfortunately, there are no liberties to escape to, unless you leave the country entirely.

Disadvantaging the young and poor

There are plenty of other ways in which government intervention disadvantages the poor. Take agriculture policy. We subsidise farm producers, but 80% of our farm subsidies go to the 25% of farmers with the largest land holdings. To protect European producers, the EU imposes high tariffs against imported farm products, which makes it impossible for farmers in poorer countries to sell their products into the EU. (That is why the EU is now the world's leading producer of beet sugar.) This policy is disastrous for countries that are dependent on a single crop, such as coffee, cocoa or sugar. It kills poor people. The tariffs are particularly stiff on processed products, blocking poorer countries from adding value by, turning their raw cocoa into chocolate and selling it to EU citizens. Nor does the policy help the European citizens, who have to pay more for their food: over £300 a year too much, according to the former Environment Secretary Owen Paterson, or maybe 20% of household food bills, according to some economists. And because food absorbs a larger share of the budget of poorer families, they are worst affected.

In 1846, after a long and bitter debate between reformers and landowners, Sir Robert Peel's government repealed the Corn Laws — restrictions on imported grain — and Britain's economy took off. Much more recently, in the 1980s, New Zealand's cash-strapped Labour government boldly scrapped farm subsidies. It incentivised farmers to diversify, innovate and raise productivity. Productivity growth doubled (even though fertiliser use halved), food prices fell and agricultural exports surged. Free trade benefits everybody. But that is *unseen*. All that is *seen* is the benefit to farmers, who naturally campaign to keep their subsidies and protections.

The streetwise economist knows that a better and simpler way of helping poorer people is to get out of their way: to remove regulations and taxes, which harm the poor most. When Alexander the Great met the Cynic philosopher Diogenes (who eschewed worldly comforts and lived in a barrel), he asked: "Great Diogenes, what can I, with all my wealth and armies, do for you?" Diogenes looked up at him and waved him away, saying: "Just stand out of the sun." And the best way for governments to help the young, the poor, and minority groups is likewise to just stand out of the sun and let them prosper on their own.

The housing crisis

Housing is another example. UK house prices are soaring, particularly in cities and in the South East, because supply is not keeping up with demand. Recently there has been net immigration of around 300,000 a year, and a trend to independent living, but the supply of new houses has not kept up with demand. That is because of all the planning regulations that prevent people building new homes, such as building height restrictions and the vast 'green belts' throttling the expansion of overcrowded cities such as London, Oxford, Cambridge and Manchester. And the 'green belt' is not even very green. Much of it is damaged land — old gravel pits, abandoned industrial workings and the like. Over a third (35%) is devoted to intensive farming, which, through the use of fertilizers, pesticides and so on, creates a net environmental *cost*. Its public amenity is zero: it is closed to the public; and wandering through vast oilseed prairies is not most people's idea of a bucolic day out anyway. Picnickers are not exactly welcome even on the 'greener' bits, like the many golf courses within the green belt around London.

While we are told that we need green belts to prevent 'urban sprawl', the fact is that Britain is far less built up than people imagine. Buildings cover about the same area that roads and railways do. And this noose around our cities makes land inside more expensive. London, for example, has the second highest property prices in the world, behind only Monaco. That in turn forces houses and shops to become smaller. New build homes are even smaller than those even in Europe's most populated county, the Netherlands. It is why UK supermarket aisles are so narrow and parking spaces in London sell for £350,000. Younger people and poorer people, who then cannot afford city-centre accommodation, instead face long journey times to and from work as they take the train or the bus through miles and miles of barren fields to the cheaper homes beyond. In addition, the tight property market makes them less mobile: they cannot move easily to take up a new job, so lose out on higher earnings. (Quite massively, according to US evidence, which suggests we could boost earnings by £10,000 per household if we built enough homes in the right places.) People also lose out because high property costs discourage firms setting up in our most dynamic cities, such as London, Manchester, Oxford and Cambridge, choking off investment from abroad and economic growth at home. Moreover, the victims of planning restrictions also have to live in cramped property where it is harder to bring up children, which partly explains why the average age at which women have their first child is now over 30. Economists calculate that the ten per cent rise in house prices in the fifteen years up to 2014 was responsible for 10,000 fewer births each year. That of course has wider implications over the years — with fewer children available to look after elderly parents, who then impose higher costs on the NHS and social care services.

The restrictive planning laws of the last fifty years have driven up UK land values four times in real terms. That has raised the ratio of house prices to earnings in London from 4:1 twenty years ago to 10:1 today. Meanwhile, rents have soared from one-fifth of renters' earnings to over a third. A recent Nationwide Building Society survey suggests it now takes the average person around nine years to save for a deposit on a home, and getting on for ten years in London. In the 1960s, the average age of a first-time buyer was 23; now it is over 30 nationwide, and 34 in some London boroughs. The government's response to their plight has been typically counterproductive: make house-buying cheaper for first-timers with special grants like Help To Buy. Such policies grab the headlines, but simply fuel demand even further, without de-restricting supply. So prices rise yet again and homes get even more unaffordable. Nor does Help To Buy actually go to the people it is meant to help. Those getting it earn an average of £55,000 nationwide and £72,000 in London – not exactly poverty rations in a country where the average household income is £25,700 – while some recipients earn as much as £100,000. Over just five years, this middle-class welfare scheme has paid out £8.3 billion to 160,000 recipients, at the poor's expense.

A streetwise economist would simply cut the red tape so as to allow more homes to be built and prices to come down. Abolishing the green belt would solve the housing crisis without any loss of amenity. As would taking intensive farms out of green belt status. Even just releasing land around rail stations would allow a million new homes to be built around London alone. The rich, in their leafy rural villages, would hardly notice. But the poor would reap a huge benefit.

Milking the school monopoly

Better-off people milk the welfare state even more systematically. You may well wonder why bricklayers in Bolton should pay higher taxes so that accountants in Ascot can school their children for nothing. And you know who is going to get the best schooling from the state education system: the families who are rich enough to move into the catchment area of a good school, where prices are higher because of that. The Nationwide reports that people pay on average £15,800 in England, and £33,000 in London, to live in the same postcode as a good secondary school rather than in the neighbouring areas. The price gap is even higher for primary schools, where it costs 8% more to live close to the best schools. If you are able to move a longer distance, the gap is higher still: it costs you £53,000 more to live near one of England's top 30 state schools, compared to the average house prices in the same county. And the premium to live near a really top state school is truly enormous: it costs nearly £300,000 extra to live near the Greycoat Hospital School in Westminster, and £330,000 more to live near the London Oratory School in Fulham, where Tony Blair sent his children.

You might conclude that such premiums for living near some of the best state secondaries are so extreme that you would be better off spending your money on private schooling instead. Not so—as the middle classes are well aware. Send your kids to a private school and they get a good education, but the money is gone. Buy a house near one of the best state schools, and they get a good education, but you get the money back when you sell the house. For those wealthy enough to exploit the system, it is a win-win. For those on the breadline, it is lose-lose. Poor areas (especially inner-city areas) tend to have poor schools, because good teachers naturally prefer nice quiet schools in nice quiet places.

It is true that parents no longer have to patronise the nearest state school. But not everyone wants to make their children travel long distances each day. And the better schools have longer application lists. A private system would simply expand to meet the demand for quality: but education is a state monopoly, directed from the centre by bureaucratic 'experts', not driven by the diverse needs of customers. Again the idea of free schools, publicly funded but independently run (often by groups set up by parents and teachers) is opening things up. In principle, at least: in fact our managerialist politicians and officials just cannot give up control. Rather than welcoming diversity, they still regulate the operations of free schools in minute detail, stifling innovation and excellence. So parents still do not get a real choice of schools that are suited to the diverse abilities (and not just the academic ability) of their children. But then those same politicians and officials are not trapped in the catchment areas of sink schools.

Free care for the rich

You might also wonder why cleaners in Cleethorpes should pay taxes to finance the health and social care of chartered accountants in Cheltenham. And again, the middle class get the best service from the state system. Professional and articulate, they know how to complain and push themselves up the waiting lists—and they have the self-confidence to do so. Many will be on first-name terms with hospital administrators and consultants.

But they are not the ones who need the service most. Life expectancy in England's most deprived areas is far less than in the richest areas — by about nine years for men and seven years for women. And not only do poorer people die earlier, they also spend more of their lives living with disease or disability — around 20 years more, on average. Obviously there are many reasons: people in poorer areas are more likely to be manual workers, and (for the reasons just mentioned above) not as well educated, or as health-aware, as those in the leafy suburbs. But the structure of (to use managerialist jargon) 'our precious' National Health Service is undoubtedly part of it. As with teachers, national pay rates mean that health professionals have no incentive to work in deprived areas, and prefer better-off places. The disparity is particularly acute in General Practitioner services, though GP surgeries are where people have most of their contacts with the NHS and where they might actually be helped and educated to take better care of their health.

The managerialist response to the continuing crises in state healthcare is to raise taxes and spend more money. That is exactly what Prime Minister Theresa May did in June 2018: officially to honour the 70th birthday of the NHS but in reality to draw the sting of her Labour critics by spending other people's money. But while more money may enable the system to deliver a bit more of everything that it delivers now, it will not change the way it works. The articulate middle classes will continue to milk the system at the expense of the poor.

Living off future generations

The state pension is a 'universal' benefit: everyone gets it. But the streetwise economist knows that richer people do better out of it, simply because (as already noted) they live longer. Indeed, pensioners as a group are better off than younger people, but they manage to procure all kinds of benefits at the expense of their children and grandchildren (and maybe others yet unborn) because politicians know that they are more likely to vote in elections.

It is another reason why so many younger and poorer people are so angry with their politicians. The National Insurance system, for example, is supposed to 'insure' people for health, social care and pensions, but it is a Ponzi pyramid scheme, passing the retired generation's expenses onto the young. The same is happening on many other fronts. Free TV licences, lower NI contributions, Winter Fuel Payments, Cold Weather Payments, Carer's Allowances that go to rich and poor alike, Housing Benefit, cheaper rail fares and free bus passes that take you anywhere in the country — all are paid for by people of working age, who know they will be lucky if the pyramid is still standing by the time they retire.

Yet pensioner households are on average £20 a week better off than working age households. They are wealthier, too, with the value of their homes rising by an average of £7,000 a year. Moreover, their pensions are rising twice as fast as the incomes of people of working age because of the 2011 'triple lock' (which boosts pensions by 2.5%, or inflation, or average earnings, whichever is highest). That policy alone imposes a cost of billions of pounds on the young. And because older people are living longer, the cost of pensions and long-term care, which younger taxpayers have to pay for, are skyrocketing. When the state pension was introduced, life expectancy was a little under 65 — so most people didn't get a pension at all. Today, a man of 65 can expect to live another 19 years, and a woman another 22.

The streetwise economist knows what managerialist politicians only fear: that it is time we restored balance and required older people to make a far greater contribution to their own generation's costs. If each generation had to pay their own way, politicians would not be able to bribe them at the polls by passing the bill for their costly perks on to the next.

8 You can see why people are angry

With managerialist government so clearly benefiting the better off and other powerful groups, while simultaneously thwarting and impoverishing the less well off and those with less electoral power, it is no surprise that people are venting their anger at the polls. The public feel that politics has gone wrong. The streetwise economist knows just how wrong.

No bonfire of controls

Before Margaret Thatcher started her programme of privatizations in 1983, the state ran all the biggest industries. My colleague, Dr Madsen Pirie, summed it up in his 'day in the life' scenario—a description of the average person's morning. When you woke up (in your state-built house) you would turn on the light (powered by state-produced electricity, generated by state-produced coal), get up and wash in state-produced water, heated by state-produced British Gas. You would pop your state-regulated Lion egg into a state-produced British Steel pan, and listen to the news on the state-run BBC radio station. (The news was mostly about strikes in the state shipbuilders or the state docks or problems in the state healthcare or postal services). You would take the kids to the state school, maybe giving a cheery wave to the state refuse collectors, before taking a state-run bus or state-run train—or possibly driving your state-produced Jaguar car—to work. And it was quite likely that you worked in a state enterprise like the state bank (in which case you might just pick up your state telephone and call in sick instead).

We still have the NHS, state schools and the BBC, of course, though many of the other industries have been privatised. But that does not mean that any of them are free of state control. On the contrary, most are controlled in minute detail by the authorities, as rail is. Buses, too: in the early 1980s, the ambition was to replace local-authority bus services—big, monopolistic, costly and inefficient—

with competing operators who would bring new ideas and new dynamism into local transport. Yet bus operations are still dominated by the local authorities, with officials deciding what services there should be, and how they should be run. Private operators merely deliver the specified service at the specified fares. It is even worse in local refuse collection services, where many of the private operators who came in, cutting costs and improving services, have been forced out and replaced by local-authority operators once again.

There is also hardly any competition in gas, water or electricity, where companies are closely regulated in terms of how they are structured, what they provide, how their pricing policy operates, and much else. There are very few phone operators too, because the UK and EU governments decide who can enter the market, what packages they can provide at what prices, what spectrum is available to whom and at what price—fundamentally a bandwith monopoly controlled by the state—and much more. Education similarly: the state funded, independently run 'free schools' are free only in name. They still have to teach and operate exactly how the local authorities and the state regulator Ofsted dictate. There are equally onerous regulations on postal services, banks, and any number of other industries.

Nor is there much public debate on the usefulness or otherwise of all this state regulation and state control, partly because the commentators who lead the public debate are themselves insiders — academics, teachers, doctors, officials, politicians and others paid by the state, and of course the broadcasters whose lives revolve around interviewing such people. There seems little point in criticising Margaret Thatcher for privatising our precious national services: they were not precious and she did not really succeed in privatising them and making them genuinely competitive.

A day in the life today

Along with the essential services we use every day, the state controls every other part of our lives too. When you wake up today, it is probably in a cramped house many miles from where you work, because of our detailed planning controls and enormous green belts. You toilet won't flush properly because of limits on the cistern size that are supposed to save the planet (though since you have to flush it twice, that hope is forlorn). Your laundry is probably still gurgling away from last night because your supposedly eco-friendly washer/drier takes an age too. When you listen to the headlines on TV or radio, you are listening to stations that need a licence from the government and whose content is strictly regulated, whether that suits you or not.

There are no cartoon characters on your cereal packet, thanks to the very vocal political campaigning by TV chef Jamie Oliver. Indeed, like cigarette 'plain packaging' it could quite easily end up covered with dire warnings that sugary cereals make you fat, complete with photographs of rotten teeth. Take your car to work and you will find it small and underpowered because carmakers must now achieve fuel efficiency targets (difficult if you are a maker that specialises in creating large luxury cars). Mind you, the poor acceleration of your car soon won't be a problem, because city streets increasingly have 20mph speed limits, imposed at the discretion of local councillors and officials, but without any national debate on the subject.

If you do not have a job but are trying to get one, you may well find yourself priced out by the National Living Wage and the cost of all those paid holidays and other time off that regulators have determined you must have, whether or not you want them. That is why getting a job depends more and more on who you know. Since it is so hard for an employer to fire you if you do not work out, they instead agree to take you on only as an intern. If you prove your worth, you will be hired: but neither side can say that. In the recent past, young people would get onto the jobs ladder by agreeing to work as an intern without pay. But you cannot do that any more because equality campaigners complained that it favoured those with rich parents. The result was that interns now have to be paid — making it hard even to get your foot on the ladder as an intern. How then are you to demonstrate your abilities to employers and get a job? That is your problem, not Whitehall's.

More patch-up regulation

As with internships, ill-conceived regulations often bring about yet further interventions as our managerialist politicians try to patch up the damage caused by their first ones. The Help to Buy scheme, intended to repair the damage of planning controls, is an example. But those second interventions often have their own unintended and damaging consequences. Help to Buy, for example, pushes up prices through the whole property chain, while its cost is funded by taxes that reduce UK competitiveness and leave ordinary people with less money.

There are legion other examples. There are so many regulations on licensed premises that it has become very expensive to drink in pubs. So instead of drinking in a controlled environment under the eye of a landlord, young people instead load up with cheap alcohol at supermarkets and get incapably drunk at home, or on the streets. After complaints from licensees about the sustainability of pubs, our managerialist Chancellor chose to give them a £1,000 business rate relief – the main effect of which is not to save pubs but merely make the tax code even more complicated then before.

Or again, after the human crush at the Hillsborough football stadium, which resulted in 96 fatalities and 766 injuries, all teams in England's top football leagues were required to install all-seater stadiums. The most enthusiastic fans still stand throughout the match, which is still dangerous: fatalities may be less likely, but injuries abound because fans frequently fall over the seats in front of them. The reduced ground capacity due to the all-seater requirement also raises the cost of tickets: by as much as £120 on the lowest-priced West Bromwich season ticket, according to research by the Adam Smith Institute. A better and cheaper solution would have been improved, safe standing areas. But our managerialist politicians, desperate to look virtuous, chose the obvious solution, whatever its real effects.

Childcare is essential to some families, particularly for single parents and those struggling on lower incomes where both parents need to work. By far the biggest cost in childcare is labour, but the regulations insist that there must be one carer for every three babies, four toddlers or eight children over three. And of course every employee comes with costs such as tax, national insurance and a raft of employee benefits. The result is that childcare has become unaffordable to those who need it most. The managerialist response is to throw taxpayers' money at the problem and spend more on subsidising childcare — rather than thinking about how to reduce the tax and regulatory barriers to affordable childcare. Norway, for example, seems to manage on a much higher ratio for the very youngest, at nine children to one carer, and France is more relaxed too. US evidence suggests that adding just one child per carer can cut costs up to 20%. And other studies show that high staff/child ratios are not just expensive, but harmful: looser rules allow carers to pay more and attract more qualified staff.

The unthinking damage

Bank regulation would be almost comic, were it not so damaging. After the financial crash, the Bank of England introduced 'stress tests' to see how the commercial banks would survive another shock. But this new regime is worse than useless, merely giving everyone false comfort. Its pass standards on capital adequacy are far too low. Valuations are done on 'book' values rather than on real, market values: so while the Bank of England thinks that the riskiness of bank assets has fallen, it has actually increased by about half. The tests are also so crude that banks can easily 'game' them. Worst of all, they pressure all banks to follow the same procedures — meaning that there is no market diversity, so that an event that ruined one bank would probably ruin them all.

Sometimes, managerialist politicians come up with proposals so potentially damaging, or so completely ill informed, that it leaves you stunned. An example is a recent suggestion to force IT firms and social media like WhatsApp to give the state access to encrypted data. The reasons given are the usual ones — we have to be able to see what criminals and terrorists are doing, and we need to protect children from pornography, radicalisation and the rest. That is the *seen* problem, and the *seen* solution seems obvious.

But there is more to it than that. For a start, if state authorities have access to our data, we are all open to blackmail. We have already seen that with medical records, where junior hospital staff have accessed the health records of well-known people and leaked them to the press. None of us would like our personal information to be leaked or even sold to the media for money by some minor state employee with access to it. That is why we protect our online activity behind passwords.

Even more remarkably, the managerialist solution of giving the authorities access to encrypted data is based on a complete misconception of how encryption works. Data are encrypted and decrypted at each end: what goes over the net is merely a fog of meaningless digits. The only way to give the authorities access would be to outlaw end-to-end encryption entirely. And that means that when you send personal information, or do online transactions at your bank, your information could be hacked by any criminal. The terrorists will simply switch to less well-known, even more secure apps like Telegram (which are important to journalists and activists facing government surveillance and censorship in countries like China and Iran). Or they will simply create their own. Hackers already invest great effort in seeking out and exploiting data weaknesses, as we saw in the 2017 WannaCry attack that shut down the IT systems at forty NHS trusts. That hack was possible because they used an old, vulnerable version of Windows: but then the NHS is a state monopoly, so such complacency was not surprising. (And, by the way, the US National Security Agency knew of the vulnerability, but didn't tell anyone, because they wanted to exploit it to spy on people.) So the *unseen* result of the proposed policy, however politically attractive it seems, is to open up all of us to extortion by criminals and the nation's infrastructure to paralysis caused by terrorists.

Gender equality regulation

Gender equality rules are another example of misguided regulation. Suppose you run a small business; it is growing fast and a new role has to be filled. You shortlist two candidates, a man and a woman, both in their early 30s. They are equally well qualified, equally capable, and equally likely to fit in. You do not really know how much you should be paying for this new role, so you ask them what they would consider a fair salary. The man asks a somewhat higher figure; but that is the only difference between them. So who do you hire? Easy, you pay the extra and hire the man, because there is a much greater probability that the woman will soon want a break from work to raise children. She will be entitled to 52 weeks off, 39 of them on 90% pay, plus her holidays and other benefits such as gym membership and health insurance. If she returns within six months you have to give her exactly the same job back — even though you might have hired someone else to plug the gap, or (since it is a fast-moving business) the same job might not even exist any more.

As our managerialist authorities seem to have realised only after putting the rules in place, all of this increases the likelihood of employers discriminating against women in their 20s and 30s. Rather than easing the regulations to make women more attractive to employers, they instead try to repair the damage by adding more. So at the job interview you are not allowed to ask things like whether someone has a steady partner, what their sexual orientation is, whether they are pregnant or aim to become so, any childcare responsibilities they have, even their age (unless that is a requirement of the job). Being only a small business, you know that you will probably not be able to keep up with all the changing gender-equality rules anyway, and could well end up in a tribunal on a discrimination charge. So why open yourself up to grief by hiring the woman? The problem is not that employers naturally discriminate — the problem is that managerialist regulation prompts them to do so.

The wider damage

Unseen, all these regulations, rules, orders, directives, conventions, ordinances, licences and laws combine to create another enterprise-crushing effect: eroding property rights, the key driver of economic growth. By restricting what people can do with their own money and property, they prevent them from using resources in the most valuable way. Instead their resources are spent on less beneficial purposes, their assets are employed less profitably, and economic growth is diminished. Everyone suffers as a result, particularly (again) the poorest. And at this deeper *unseen* level, personal responsibility — accepting the consequences of your own action — is diminished, because it is the managerialist authorities who decide how you should act, not you.

Remember also that the officials who draft regulations and run public industries are risk-averse. They are charged with spending the public's money wisely, not venturing it on risky opportunities, as an entrepreneur does. And this risk-aversion is reflected in how regulations are drafted and public services are run. Regulations become more and more detailed and onerous, because the regulators' interest is to prevent mess-ups — whatever that costs others. State-run operations are rarely innovative, because innovation means risk. It all means fewer opportunities are grasped and the public get a worse, more costly service from both private and public providers.

By killing innovation, regulation hurts us all. Often the rules are written in terms of existing technologies, making the adoption of new, better methods impossible. The same with working practices: the courts ruled that according to the law, Uber drivers and others in the gig economy should get minimum pay, paid holidays and other rights enjoyed by full-time workers. Our relatively flexible labour market (compared with Continental Europe) has allowed the UK to created two million new private sector jobs since 2010, while job growth on the Continent has been flat; it allows firms like Uber and Deliveroo to create innovative new employment models that give workers and customers more choices and opportunities. But regulating away the freedoms of the gig economy seems a sure way of blocking technological progress, which will be welcomed by established firms such as licensed taxi drivers, but not by customers.

In the case of taxis, such attempts at control will merely hasten the development of driverless vehicles. But no doubt the existing interests will seek ways to stop those too. The regulator Transport for London, for example, tried to revoke Uber's licence to operate in the capital, even though around 3.5m Londoners regularly use Uber because it is cheaper, safer and quicker. Its 40,000 drivers choose the app because it gives them total flexibility, and the average driver earns £12 an hour after costs, well over the National Living

Wage. But then black cab drivers are represented on the Transport for London and Uber drivers are not. Uber had to go to court to get the ban reversed.

In the case of taxis, such attempts at control will merely hasten the development of driverless vehicles. But no doubt the existing interests will seek ways to stop those too

State-approved lifestyles

It is not just the economy that is stifled by regulation. In an age of interest-group politics, it is the most messianic of interest groups that dominate the debate. Businesspeople who seek commercial protections have nothing on the zealots who believe they know what is best for us and are willing to use the power of the state to make sure we get it.

Take the campaigns against fatty food. Public Health England, a quango, wants targets to limit calories in pizzas, burgers and ready meals — backed up by the state's regulatory power over providers. But people eat pizzas and burgers because they taste good, and ready meals because they are quick and easy. They know they are fattening. Making pizzas less cheesy or burgers smaller (for probably the same price) cheats us of both value and pleasure.

The same quango says that a 20% tax on sugary drinks would save 77,000 lives in the next quarter century — a truly remarkable claim to clairvoyance, but wrong. At the *seen* level, perhaps it might reduce people's consumption of taxed drink, though in Mexico and France, where it has been tried, it has had scant effect, except (as Lucozade found out with its disastrous new 'low sugar' recipe) in ruining people's enjoyment. Fizzy drinks do not seem to cause obesity anyway: even though we are getting heavier, we are downing fewer of them. US soft drink consumption is at a 30-year low, and it has been falling in the UK too.

There are wider *unseen* effects too. As a consumption tax, a sugar tax hits poorer people hardest (once again): richer people won't even notice it. Since fruit- and milk-based drinks are excluded, the tax is likely to drive people to other sugar-heavy drinks — like orange juice—just as high taxes on cigarettes drive people to stronger, higher-tar brands. And as the Institute for Fiscal Studies has said, people will probably consume other products such as yoghurt and chocolate to keep up their sugar intake. It is governments that are the junkies: once they have got used to the tax revenues, they will be unable to give them up.

Cigarette 'plain packaging' is hardly plain, as it has features pictures of diseased lungs. We wait to see its results. After Australia introduced it, there was no fall in tobacco spending at all: indeed, scholars at RMIT University in Melbourne found that spending actually increased. That must come as a relief to Treasury officials, who do not want to lose the whopping £12 billion brought in by tobacco tax. Even with the £3bn-£6bn cost of NHS treatment for smokers, that is a healthy profit.

Meanwhile, EU regulators could not decide how to treat new tobacco products, such as vape and heat-not-burn alternatives. Some wanted them 'medicalised' — they would be covered by reams of pharmaceuticals regulation, and you would need a prescription to get them. In the event, Brussels decided to regulate them like cigarettes and other nicotine products—even though it is the smoke, not the nicotine, that is harmful: e-cigarettes do only 1%-5% of the harm of conventional ones. The Office of National Statistics discovered that e-cigarettes do not turn people into conventional cigarette smokers: actually, they are the best way to wean smokers off the killer sticks. In Japan, where heat-not-burn e-cigarettes are openly advertised, their market share has risen to 10% of nicotine products, and cigarette sales plummeted by 12.4% last year. In Australia, where e-cigarettes are banned, the proportion of the population who smoke cigarettes dropped by just 0.6 percentage points in the three years up to 2016. Sadly, regulation kills.

Regulation and corruption

The bigger the state, and the more extensive its interventions, the greater scope there is for corruption. Perhaps a few favours or political donations here and there might secure a subsidy or tax concession, or get you round some regulatory obstacle. But it is not necessarily financial corruption, which (despite question marks over the honours system) is comparatively rare in the UK. There are other forms too, like who do you know who owns a rent-controlled lease they can pass on to you, or what council official can bump you up the housing list, or what friendly doctor can shorten your wait for treatment, or which MP can shortcut your passport application? Or maybe, can you get yourself onto a regulatory quango so that you can keep innovative new competitors out of your business sector, or onto one of the remuneration committees created by company regulators, which are supposed to make executive pay more transparent but in fact provide useful back-scratching opportunities?

As well as rent *seeking* by those trying to get special favours from politicians, government power also encourages rent *selling*. King John blatantly sold judicial judgements. Edward III's chums William Latimer (Chamberlain) and Richard Lyons (Warden of the Mint) took bribes for favours. Stuart and Tudor monarchs had a nice earner in selling monopolies. But today the process has become subtler. For example, politicians may threaten an industry with regulation, then wait for party donations or other favours to come in before withdrawing the threat. And the prospect of a knighthood or peerage can be very enticing to a business leader who might be persuaded to make a party donation.

The best way to get rid of corruption in high places is to get rid of high places. But the managerialist response is to deal with the problem by enacting yet more regulations. A recent example is the complicated and costly regulations to register lobbyists, and to monitor the activity of public affairs firms, trade associations and advocacy groups. Nobody stops to reflect that lobbying only exists because government is such a large potential source of favours and money. The streetwise economist knows that cutting down government would be far more effective than building up regulation—and a lot better in terms of keeping our rights and our money safe.

Stop thinking of it as *your* money

If you do get a job and want to save up for a small, cramped, faraway home of your own, you face taxes on your income, taxes on your job, taxes on almost everything you spend, taxes on your enjoyments such as alcohol and fizzy drinks, taxes on your car and the fuel you put into it, taxes on your electricity bill, taxes on your airline travel, taxes on your insurance bills, taxes on just happening to live somewhere, and taxes on the home you eventually are able to afford. If you do manage to save any money, you are taxed on the interest, even if you lose most of it through inflation. You are even taxed on giving your money away or leaving it to your friends and family when you die. You do not even see much of this tax — as when Gordon Brown, as Chancellor, loaded an extra £15bn-worth of additional 'stealth' taxes on to taxpayers. It is a case of "plucking the goose so as to procure the largest amount of feathers with the least amount of hissing," as Louis XIV's finance minister Jean-Baptiste Colbert once put it.

The trick, though, is to stop thinking of it as *your* money, because it isn't — or not for long, at least. The UK government takes around two-fifths of everything we earn. Each year, we work 148 days of the year exclusively for the government. That is from 1 January to around 29 May — dubbed 'Tax Freedom Day'. This tax burden, £700bn in total, is bigger than any time since the early 1980s. In 2000, just 1.7 million of us paid the 40p income tax rate. By 2010, that was up, to 3 million. Now it is 4.3 million. Many more on £100,000+ have been dragged into tax income rates of over 60p. At this rate, it may soon be bigger than any time since the late 1970s.

Even then, that is not enough to satisfy our rulers, so they borrow. Not as much as in previous decades, certainly, but still nearly two percent of the nation's income, year on year on year. Add in all that borrowing, which you and your children will pay for soon enough, and you find yourself slaving for the government until mid-June. Taxwise, we are worse off than mediaeval serfs, who only had to work about a third of the time for their feudal lords. ("Ane tae saw, ane tae graw, and ane to pay the laird witha'" as Scots peasants used to say.) They were lucky. If our governments really wanted economic growth instead of just managing the country's economic decline, they would start thinking of ways to reduce tax and borrowing, not to keep on increasing them.

Stop thinking of it as *your* life

If you can still afford a home of your own, not only will it be small, cramped and faraway, it will also be made more expensive by an enormous rulebook of building regulations. These cover the plans that have to be submitted in advance, the use of the building, the materials used and how they are installed, the utilities used, the electrics, its energy efficiency, its water use, ventilation, fire proofing, sound insulation, heat insulation and much else, even down to the spacing of the banisters and the height of electricity sockets on the wall. And the person selling you the house will have to produce detailed information including surveys and heat efficiency ratings. Nobody really knows how many thousands of pages of all this stuff there are, but following the rules is a costly business, and another reason it takes people decades to save for a deposit. If you buy an old house with a garden, you'd better like trees because they could well have a preservation order on them. Even if they drain your garden dry and condemn it to perpetual umbra, the council won't sympathise. Your only hope is to find a former council tree preservation officer who is now a consultant and gets paid to find ways around the rules that they formerly enforced – another nice little earner for those on the inside.

If you decide to go out for a drink to take your mind of all this taxation and regulation, you should be on your best behaviour. The police routinely oppose applications for pub and restaurant licences unless CCTV is installed. That is one reason why we now have up to 5.9 million CCTV cameras, according to the British Security Industry Association – without any public debate whatsoever. You cannot smoke in the pub even if the owners and other customers do not mind. And if you smoke outside, do not throw away the stub without thinking or you could get a £60 on-the-spot littering fine.

You could smoke in your own car – provided you do not give a lift to anyone under 18 or use it as a taxi. That is, if your car has not been confiscated and crushed by the police for some other offence. (Or sold, since the police can profit from selling your property, another nice little earner for those with state power.) And since the police are rewarded partly on their arrest statistics, you should count them as part of the problem, rather than the solution. Not the guardians of your rights and freedoms, but the state's paid enforcers, routinely armed with automatic weapons (no public debate on that, either).

You need to be streetwise to stay free in a country that is free only in name.

9 Managing away our cash and our rights

Disparaging the golden goose

When Jeremy Corbyn, John McDonnell and their colleagues attack economic freedom, they have an open goal. There is an old joke that the trouble with the profit system — (at least in its current, politics-dominated incarnation) — is that not enough people profit from it. People think it benefits only the better off. That should not and need not be true. Still, given the prosperity that capitalism has brought the world, even in its current cronyist form, it has surprisingly many critics and surprisingly few defenders.

Unfortunately you cannot expect businesspeople to defend capitalism. With the power and patronage of managerialist politicians up for grabs, their rational interest lies in getting protections and favours for themselves, and keeping out the competition. And even if businesspeople do support free markets in general, they are hands-on practitioners of capitalism, not slick advocates for it. So the criticisms persist that 'capitalists' are greedy, cutthroat and over-powerful.

To a streetwise economist, that view is completely wrong. Yes, a free economy is based on people's natural self-interest: we work, invent, produce, and sell in order to benefit ourselves and our families. But self-interest is not the same as greed. Free and competitive markets punish greed. Nobody goes back to a supplier they think has given them or their friends a poor deal. Producers can't live on a 'quick buck': they need customers who will come back time and again, and recommend their product to others.

Nor can businesspeople afford to be cutthroat. The most successful ones are not heartless exploiters. Business is a long-term activity, based on long-term relationships. You cannot afford to keep falling out with workers, suppliers and customers and scrabbling around for new ones. You cannot get the best from people unless you treat them with respect.

As for business being powerful, governments have more power in their little finger. A business cannot make you fight wars, tax you, spend your money, direct your life, and throw you in jail. Despite all the talk of 'big business', small businesses are 2,000 times more numerous and employ five times as many people. The only time when businesses have too much power is when politicians give it to them in the form of favours and subsidies that protect them from competition.

The great enrichment

Capitalism, left to its own devices, has delivered the world enormous prosperity. In the millennia from ancient Egypt to the Industrial Revolution of the 1760s, human life changed little. Most people spent their days producing food. In 1800, the US economic historian Deirdre McCloskey (1942) calculates, the average citizen of the world had an income between $1 and $5 a day. Now it averages nearly $50 a day. Even that masks big differences: while some of the world's most anti-capitalist societies (e.g. Central African Republic, Congo, North Korea) languish on $5 a day or less, earnings in capitalist Switzerland, Australia and even the UK are over $90 a day. Americans pocket over $100 a day.

Nor is this confined to the few. In 1800, decent housing, sanitation, lighting, heating, travel, leisure, fresh meat and fruit were luxuries for the rich. Now they are affordable to everyone in developed countries, and growing numbers of people in developing ones. That is because the capitalist exchange economy is so hugely productive. Hardly anyone had spare clothes until the power looms of the Industrial Revolution made them cheap and plentiful. The science author Matt Ridley (1958-) calculates that today's electric lights provide illumination 43,200 times more cheaply than the candles of 1800, while farm production is 600 times higher. Smartphones, another miracle of capitalism, enable around two billion people to talk to friends, pull down vast libraries of information, and do business with others on the far side of the world.

None of this happened because technological advances are somehow inevitable. It happened because capitalism provides the incentives for people to make such advances and reap the rewards from happy customers. Thirty years of open trade, markets, liberalisation and deregulation have done far more to eliminate human poverty than a century of Lenin, Stalin, Mao, Pol Pot, Mugabe and Chavez. In 1990, says the World Bank, about 40% of the human population lived on less than $1.90 a day; today it is less than 10%. Poverty has been cut more in the last 30 years than in the last 3,000.

The meaning of capital

Despite all those achievements, you cannot expect our managerialist rulers to defend capitalism. They rather enjoy their power and patronage over 40% of the economy and 100% of our lives. And like most people, they do not really understand the workings of capitalism and the nature of capital. They cannot see past the propagandist clutter that critics have loaded onto the 'capitalism' concept: greed, heartlessness, monopoly, satanic mills and all the rest.

But *capitalism* is actually a simple concept. The word has two parts. *Capital* is just the tools, equipment, plant, resources, networks, and systems that we build up in order to make production easier, cheaper and more efficient. And *ism* just means that this is a general way of life: not surprisingly, since producing useful goods and services is vital to us, and we want to do it with the least cost and effort possible.

But *capital* does not just exist. You have to create it by saving for it and investing in it—giving up your time, and foregoing a bit of current enjoyment, in order to build or buy a tool that will make you more productive in the future. It could mean acquiring a computer so that you can manage your customer accounts more easily; or a machine that manufactures your product in a hundredth of the time; or savings that help you ride out changing fortunes. It is our use of such capital goods that make us, and capitalism, so productive.

The democracy of capital

Far from being the prerogative of a rich few, capital is remarkably democratic. Take *financial capital*, so hated of capitalism's critics. It is the oil that makes all those machines and factories run. Businesses that make customers happier generate more income: consequently they can offer investors better returns, and attract more investment; so financial capital flows into its most productive uses, and away from less productive ones. That is a huge positive for us all. But the capital that these markets move around does not belong to a wealthy few. Its ultimate owners are mostly ordinary people who save in their bank, building society or pension accounts. That is, nearly all of us.

And there is another form of capital that we *all* own: what economists call *human capital* – the personal qualities that make us productive individuals. It includes our knowledge, education and skills, and even qualities such as being conscientious or looking after our health. We *invest* in those things, just as we might invest in computers or savings accounts, to make ourselves more productive. We go to college or night school to learn skills that will earn us higher rewards; we teach our children self-discipline, reliability, punctuality and other traits that will help their careers; and employers invest time and money to train their staff. Adding all that up, *human capital* contributes more to production than every other form of capital combined. But this is capital that *everyone* owns.

Furthermore, we all benefit from other people's capital every time we buy goods and services. We do not have to make ourselves experts in plumbing, electrics, accounting, car repairs or dentistry; we can go to other people who have acquired these skills and have invested in the tools needed to practise them. We buy groceries, phones, clothes, washer-driers, cars or pianos that other people's skills, equipment and networks deliver to us at thousandths of the cost of doing it ourselves – if we ever could produce these things ourselves.

So the *capital* that makes capitalism so incredibly productive is also hugely democratic. All of us have a bit of human capital; nearly all of us have a stake in financial capital; and we all benefit from the human, financial and physical capital of others. When ideologues attack 'capital' and 'capitalists', they are actually attacking all of us.

A moral system

Those same ideologues speak as if their vision has a monopoly on virtue, saying that while capitalism is about greed and selfishness, socialism is about shared purposes, altruism and the common good. That vision might just hold up in a family or small group where shared purposes are easily agreed. But it cannot possibly work in our large, worldwide society in which different people have widely diverse purposes, philosophies and methods. Who decides what the 'common good' is, and what the 'shared purpose' should be? How do they know that this is the right purpose? And how do they force doubters and dissidents to participate in realising it? Those obvious questions demonstrate why socialism so often morphs into tyranny.

Actually, you can make a much more compelling case for the moral virtue of capitalism. It rejects force and exploitation. It allows us all to pursue our own purposes freely and peacefully. It is based on mutual service and reciprocity. It rewards people who satisfy others' needs most cost-effectively. It encourages the efficient use of effort and resources. It promotes specialisation, which raises productivity and encourages diversity. That diversity in turn promotes toleration and respect for different people and lifestyles, not to mention greater care for them as individuals rather than as cogs in the collective machine. And growing wealth allows yet further philanthropy through charities, churches, clubs and the other voluntary associations of civil society.

Even money itself is a moral construct. Money is simply a promise, an IOU for future services. You accept it in payment for your goods and services because you are confident that you can exchange it for the goods or services you might need at some unspecified point in the future. Money would have no purpose or value if you could not trust people to honour that future promise. Money is built on trust; it encourages us to be trustworthy and to trust others. And it makes reciprocation and collaboration easy by serving as a medium of exchange—so hungry barbers do not have to search for bakers in need of a haircut, as the American economist Milton Friedman put it.

"Run for your life from any man who tells you that money is evil," advised Ayn Rand. "That sentence is the leper's bell of an approaching looter."

A resilient system

Capitalism is resilient precisely because it is so useful to us. It wasn't killed by the 2008-9 financial crash, as Marxists crowed at the time. (But then they predicted capitalism's demise in every one of the 190-odd downturns that one country or another has suffered since Marx wrote *Das Kapital* — though nearly all of those were over within a year, and nearly all the rest in two. It is only our modern governments' ineptitude that makes them last longer today.)

Capitalism not only adapts to changing events; it even absorbs natural and financial disasters. Say an earthquake destroys many homes. The price of houses then goes up; people share accommodation or live in smaller apartments; the higher price induces more builders to construct more homes; everyone can find a new home and the price falls again. Or say there is a run on a bank. The bank suspends payments until it can rebuild its reserves; or other banks step in and buy its good business, leaving its bad bits to go bust; shareholders and bondholders take a hit, but banking goes on. Every time you think it must be dead, capitalism breaks through the tarmac.

Compare that with events in a managerialist economy. Some event provokes a housing shortage; property owners start charging higher rents; governments then intervene, capping rents to keep them 'affordable' — and we are back in the rent-control miasma again. Nobody builds new rented homes, landlords take their property off the market or let it crumble, it gets harder for people to find appropriate accommodation, and the crisis gets even worse. Or take another example. A bank fails; the government bails it out with taxpayers' money; it limps on, crippled by its bad loans; others figure they can take crazy risks too, keeping the cash if they succeed and letting taxpayers bail them out if they do not; nobody gets rid of their bad debts, government forces them to merge in order to spread the risk; competition is reduced; there is even less pressure to jettison bad business; and the chance of an even bigger catastrophe is increased. (We saw precisely that in both the US and UK not too long ago.)

Capitalism adapts to changing events. It is not an unbending enforcer of some preconceived political plan. But it is easily corrupted by the political system and the power of the state over it. In trying to protect the public, politicians crowd out the much better regulator that is market competition. Or they give in to noisy lobbyists who convince them of the need to keep out ('cowboy') competitors. They might even be corrupt. But the end result is the same: too much monopoly and too little competition, in banking, finance, manufacturing, retail, land ownership and everything else. This managerialist style of capitalism is no advertisement for the real thing. A streetwise person looks behind the *seen* policies through to the *unseen* corrupting effects.

The complacency of Westerners

When you control economic life, you control all life. There can be no political freedom, for example, where all of the main media outlets are controlled by the state. How could you even organise a political meeting if the state controls social media, phone networks, transport, meeting venues, and more?

It is remarkable how easily a managerialist state can erode our fundamental rights, such as life, liberty, property, free speech and assembly. That is because we in the English-speaking world have enjoyed those rights for so long that they are part of our very consciousness. Our whole history has been the story of our struggles to create them, assert them, defend them or restore them. Over centuries, we have built up the institutions that embody and preserve them, such as parliamentary democracy, the rule of law, habeas corpus, jury trial, due process and limited government. The security they give us has enabled us to build up our physical, human and cultural capital in peace, and so to create wealth and prosper.

We have become so used to these rights and institutions that we do not even notice them. People in other countries live each day under rulers who use state power to enrich themselves and their cronies, who have judges in their pockets, who throw critics into jail, who use violence to maintain control, who shut down newspapers and block websites, who persecute homosexuals and others they disapprove of—and much else. But our own rights and institutions make us so secure from such abuse that we can scarcely believe such things could happen.

That makes us particularly vulnerable when our own rights and institutions are undermined. We cannot imagine their loss, and think that nothing can dent our security. So, even as our rights are compromised, we do not bother to resist. We might even cheer, not seeing how crucial our rights of property, law, justice, free speech and limited government are to our very freedom.

Violating our rights

For example, trial by jury—hinted at in Magna Carta (1215) and consolidated into our constitution over subsequent centuries—is an essential safeguard. It means you cannot be fined, jailed or killed on the order of any political authority: you can be convicted only by a panel of ordinary people like yourself. But now, governments argue that jury trials are too expensive, especially for minor crimes; and that we cannot expect ordinary citizens to sit through very long trials as jurors, nor understand very complex ones. So this principle, many centuries and deaths in the making, is simply managed out of existence for financial and administrative convenience.

The same has happened to the right of silence, established in common law from the 17th century. Again, it is (or was) a powerful protection for innocent people who may have been led under interrogation to say things that might prejudice their trial. But the managerialists complained that the right helped terrorists and 'professional criminals' who could simply refuse to answer any questions at all. So now, your trial *is* prejudiced by your silence. Indeed, your right to silence no longer applies at all in some trials. You also have to disclose encryption keys, say who was driving if your vehicle is involved in an offence, and give your name if a police officer thinks you're acting in an 'anti-social' manner. Any of these things might seem reasonable in particular cases; but all are violations of a principle of *unseen* but vital importance.

In these any many, many other ways (such as politicians seeking to open up *everyone's* online activity to official scrutiny), our *unseen* protections are routinely violated for passing matters of *seen* expediency. We live in a country that is free only in name. Only the streetwise will survive.

The immoral state

Our right to own private property and to decide what we do with it is of course long gone. Two-fifths of what we produce is taken in taxes for purposes that the managerialists think appropriate. We all know the moral case that taxes are needed to pay for vital public services. But that argument is not so convincing when these services are systematically exploited by the better off. There are moral shortcomings of taxation too.

Taxes may be a *necessary* evil, but they are still an evil. They are extracted from us by force: if you do not pay, you go to jail. But using force is undesirable—even if the government does it. Perhaps force is justifiable if it produces a better outcome. But does it? While most people would gladly pay taxes for things like defence, policing, justice, vital infrastructure and maybe a few welfare benefits, they still think they could spend most of the money better themselves. And it is hardly moral to take people's money by force if it is wasted by bureaucrats or guzzled by the interest groups who dominate spending decisions.

Taxation also forces people to pay for things that offend their moral principles. In commercial markets, different people can choose different things. But public policy decides things for everyone: and that choice may well violate some people's deeply held beliefs. They may object to mixed-sex schools, for example, or believe that foreign wars and abortion are state-sponsored murder done in their name. But politicians arrogate these moral choices to themselves. Moreover, taxes leave people with less to spend on their own moral and philanthropic choices. People in (the lower taxed) US give more than twice as much to schools, hospitals, libraries, galleries, orchestras and welfare charities than people in the UK.

When people see taxes as high and unjustified, they seek to shift the burden to others: usually 'the rich'. This has succeeded: the top 1% of income tax payers earn 12% of the nation's income, but pay nearly 30% of the total take. Such envy taxation is not just morally corrosive, it is also economically damaging: these days, most of 'the rich' get rich by producing goods and services that benefit others — not by merely inheriting wealth. Taxing them throttles that creativity.

High taxes are also morally corrosive in that they prompt people to avoid or evade them. The predictable managerialist response to this — tightening the rules further — breeds even greater resentment, and feeds the cycle. The US comic Will Rogers once said that income tax had made more liars out of Americans than golf. When even professionals ask whether you would like to pay in cash rather than pay VAT, and homebuyers routinely offer vast amounts for 'fittings' rather than pay stamp duty on the full value of a property, you know that taxes have corrupted us all.

High taxes make liars out of politicians and officials too. Rather than come clean about the amount of tax they are extracting, they rely on stealth taxes to conceal the burden — fiddling income thresholds, not adjusting for inflation, changing rules and reliefs on pensions, putting unseen taxes on insurance or air travel, and much more. And the bigger the state, the more people that work for it, and the more people who have an interest in keeping it big. Roughly 60% of people's income in Scotland derives from public spending. In the North-East of England, it is more than 70%. In Wales, nearly 80%. No wonder they vote for high-spending politicians. And no wonder the rest of the country reckons we have been well and truly stitched up by the big-state mob.

Farewell to free speech

If you think these worries are exaggerated, look at what has happened to free speech. Jeremy Corbyn has said that the press is not free because "it is controlled by billionaire tax exiles". His "change is coming" remark was a clear hint that if he became Prime Minister he would make newspapers sign up to his approved regulator or hit them with paying the costs for both sides in libel or privacy claims. Even the *Guardian* called it "the most explicit attack by a senior politician in modern times on the philosophical underpinning of press ownership." So a free press is fine, as long as politicians approve of the owners and can control what they print. And since news is increasingly moving online, there is no obvious point at which such government control might stop (even control of the internet, which is already starting to happen).

Free speech exists for many good reasons. It allows people to criticise the authorities without fear of reprisal. If citizens can debate public policy openly, that will probably lead to better policy. Free speech enables new ideas to come forward, which is vital to future progress. Even if the vast majority of the population disagree with those ideas, there may be truth in them. And existing ideas need to be challenged if they are to remain robust.

Of course, free speech does not justify inciting violence against anyone, nor reckless language that risks physical injury — like shouting 'Fire!' in a crowded theatre, as the nineteenth-century philosopher John Stuart Mill noted. But Mill's exceptions covered only *physical* injury. They did not prohibit things that others might say is *psychologically* distressing — like name-calling, racial abuse, or expressing support for nasty ideologies — because such alleged hurt is invisible, and cannot be measured. It would simply give people an excuse to silence their critics. Yet today, people use precisely that justification for precisely that end.

For example, schoolteacher and Labour Party member Roy Wilkes was accused by his own trade union, the National Union of Teachers, of "grossly discriminating (transphobic) statements...that were damaging to the mental health of members". Actually, his words were pretty innocuous and he beat the rap. But it is remarkable that using words that other people do not want to hear is now evidence that you have a phobia (which is a mental disorder). And how can you possibly defend yourself against claims of damaging someone else's mental health? How could you prove that you hadn't?

The Street-wise Guide to the British Economy

Or again, our colleges and universities should be bastions of free speech, since only when ideas are contested can we test their validity, which is how learning advances. But where academics and students once honed their critical faculties by freely debating all kinds of controversial (even outrageous) ideas, universities now routinely 'no-platform' people whose views they disagree with. When I addressed the Oxford University Hayek Society, formed to explore the ideas of the twentieth-century liberal scholar and Nobel economist F. A. Hayek, I had to do so in a local pub, because the organiser's college, St Hugh's, ruled that such liberal ideas were too distressing to be discussed on its property.

I guess that is what happens when 75% of academics lean Left and communicate their prejudices to their unworldly students. Meanwhile, the students of King's College Cambridge fly a Hammer & Sickle flag over the college bar—which is utterly contemptible, given the appalling human cost of that ideology. But rather than retire to a safe space, we should criticise them, even as we uphold their right to fly whatever flag they want. I wonder if they would uphold the same freedom, if someone else wanted to fly, say, the Swastika.

The right to free speech does protect you from criticism and contempt, nor mean that you must be taken seriously. You can ban anyone you like from your own home. But on the public property that is a university (financed by taxpayers, supposedly in order to expand minds, not close them), free speech should prevail. And the more property that is controlled by state organisations, the less safe space (to coin a phrase) there is for open discussion. Let's hope they do not nationalise the pubs.

It is dopamine politics: we must only say things that make folk feel good. The vital principle of free speech is violated in the name of niceness. So you can be jailed for saying rude things about racial groups, or handing out Christian leaflets near a mosque, or countless other 'hate' crimes. But this all confuses morality and law. If people use bigoted language, we should be arguing against them and calling for tolerance, not locking them up.

In early 2018, the police detained an Alt-Right speaker who intended to spout his views at Speakers Corner in Hyde Park, on the ground that socialist groups had threatened disruption. In such cases, it should be the threat-makers that are arrested, not the speaker: otherwise, intolerant people could stop anyone saying anything they do not like, merely by threatening violence. But when you look at the conduct in our universities, on our streets and at our elections, perhaps this has already happened.

Maybe liberal-minded individuals should use the same tactics: saying we cannot allow people to defend communism because it distresses us so much. But then we are not trying to silence views we disagree with — only to expose them to criticism. A genuine response to the censorship cult requires a firm understanding of the purpose and principles of free speech. That is something that managerialist politicians, media and intellectuals rarely have.

Conceding freedom to the state

On such slippery slopes, our freedoms are lost. It is easy to convince people that drugs, sugar or tobacco must be curbed because they damage our health or corrupt children. It violates the liberal principle that people should be free to make their own lifestyle choices, but then the exceptions are *seen* and the wider value of the principle is *unseen*. Often, the regulations will not achieve the stated end anyway. They might well lead to worse horrors (such as drug gang warfare). Sometimes they have the opposite effect to that intended.

It is easy to point to cases where people say things that seem likely to cause distress to others, and then to assault the principle of free speech. But because almost everyone agrees that there must be *some* exceptions, we should be even more careful about violating the principle further. Our freedom to act, argue and even to think may depend on it.

It is rational to panic

Past generations have been well aware of how such breaches of principle can segway into wholesale violations of our fundamental and vital freedoms. And there are plenty of unconventional politicians around who would have no problem with that at all. Is it time we started to panic?

The crucial advice to space travellers in *The Hitchhiker's Guide To The Galaxy* was "Don't Panic!" But here on Earth, panic seems (in the words of another TV space traveller, Mr Spock) "perfectly rational". Panic is how streetwise people avoid trouble. You see a gang of young men loitering on the corner. Your senses prickle. It is a visceral yet rational response to a threat—one that could spare you a mugging. So you turn back. Trouble averted.

The political threats are all round. Our political sector has expanded. Politics seems to be all our TV news channels talk about—but then they are part of the same managerial nexus. Even natural disasters are traced back to 'the cuts' or some other political question. The managerialist Leviathan dips at will into our money, intervenes in our lifestyle and suspends our rights for its convenience. It fetishises 'democratic' action so much that democracy is buckling under the weight of all its laws and regulations. It is self-perpetuating, run by and for the benefit of a separate class.

Alienated by all this, the public look for alternatives, many of which turn out to be just as statist, without any of the liberalism. Authoritarian radicals like Momentum get within striking distance of power, happy to tear up an economic system that spreads prosperity to the poorest, and replace it with another that brought only tyranny, famine and genocide. They use the language of public health, or terrorism, or child protection as reasons to scrap our rights and safeguards, which they know stand in the way of their collective action. Only the streetwise realise the *unseen* dangers.

ESCAPING A BAD NEIGHBOURHOOD

10 A brighter future

If we are to escape the grim economic and political neighbourhood we are in, we need to have a vision of where we want to be instead.

First, though, we have to convince our neighbours — who have got used to the mean streets we inhabit, and that we would be better off somewhere else. But that is getting pretty obvious. Much of the Western world is in political turmoil, with people turning to third parties, nationalists and demagogues. Our political system has brought us economic turmoil, with a damaging crash and recession brought on by incompetent state regulation, bad monetary management, official complacency and too much focus on pursuing the *seen* rather than on understanding the *unseen*. Economic growth has been weak, or even negative in some countries and some periods. And yet government budgets seem unable to cope with the demand put on them. Borrowing has soared, while budgets are being squeezed. We are definitely in a bad neighbourhood.

But that is not because we have become somehow morally weak or corrupt. It is because our political system breeds such problems. It feeds the self-interest of voters, rent-seekers, politicians, news media and officials. It serves this mutually reinforcing, professionalised class, rather than the public, who have become disaffected and estranged. And it feeds on itself, fetishising democratic (that is, political) decision-making until nearly everything becomes beholden to government. A bigger state means more spoils to lobby over, insiders work the system at the expense of the outsiders and the poor, and policy becomes ever more distorted and unprincipled. Policymakers focus on the *seen* and the sellable, while the *unseen* reality is progressively damaged. Taxes creep higher and regulation infiltrates deeper, innovation is stifled, competition is reduced, economic growth falters, controls harden, property and other personal rights are eroded, and the public are left exposed and alienated, thrashing around for almost any alternative.

Which way out?

People vote against politicians, not for them. But the populist and nationalist parties and demagogues who want to replace the managerialists are rarely a sound alternative. On the contrary, they are often just as controlling and those they would replace. Nor, plainly, are Jeremy Corbyn, John McDonnell and their supporters a sound choice. They have brought state socialism back from the dead, postwar-style nationalisation out of the policy vaults, and old-style tax and spend policies into discussion again. But it was those politics that got us into this dangerous neighbourhood; and when the Conservatives try to defuse them by offering us merely a lower-octane equivalent, our neighbourhood gets even darker.

We need to be frank about the failures of state socialism, and its ruinous cost in terms of both prosperity and human life. And we must not be deflected by the argument that it was not 'real' socialism, for it was. Socialism implies a collective agenda, a single vision for society; but that can be achieved only by silencing the dissenters and stifling all other visions. Your rights of property, free speech, action and even thought must be subjugated to the chosen purpose. No wonder it ends in purges – and poverty too, since no central planner can possibly understand and process the hugely diverse needs, wants, resources, methods, networks, products and services of a modern productive nation.

Equally we need to be positive about capitalism – even if we call it something else because of the baggage that its critics have loaded the word with. We have to assert that the profit system works and that profit is good – it simply means getting more value out than you put in, something we all strive for every day. And in an open and competitive economy, the only way to create profit is by serving others, who will gladly reward you for the benefit you bring them. (Contrast that happy outcome with the crony economy, in which profits can be made by extracting favours from insider friends.) We need to explain too that capital is not a fixed resource but has to be created. That it is not some privilege of the rich but something nearly everyone has, in their minds, bodies and savings. That we build up capital because it makes us so very much more productive—as well as adaptable and resilient to changing events.

You cannot expect business people to make this case. Nor will academics and intellectuals be supporters, since the state is usually their paymaster. Even the politicians who believe in a free society and free economy are likely to be too absorbed by the opinion polls to develop a principled vision of a smaller state, lower taxes, widespread property ownership and strong individual rights. (Which might explain why Conservative membership has halved in the last ten years, while Labour membership has trebled.)

Nor is our escape helped by the general complacency about our situation. Our rights and legal protections, bought with blood, are watered down in the name of expediency and we hardly notice, or even welcome it. It is therefore no easy task to convince the millions who are stuck in a bad place and need to get out. Only a principled vision of something better is likely to convince them. So it is with the principles of a free economy and free society that we must start.

The principles for escape

In a free society, government is limited: most of life is independent of it. This is not just the old Indian joke: 'The economy grows at night—when the government is sleeping.' It means that the government has no role at all in most of the activities that are really important to people. It does not intervene on actions and interactions that are purely voluntary. It is there to protect people against fraud, theft and force so that they can interact on the basis of trust.

A free society sees the individual as more important than the collective. It would not sacrifice the individual's freedom for the collective benefit, nor use force against individuals, without some really overwhelming reason to do so. And it would be for those who want to intervene to make the case. A free society does not simply assume it has power over individuals, their money and their property. It uses strictly limited, representative government to make those few collective decisions that individuals cannot make themselves. It respects people's property, and their freedom to trade it as they choose, as the basis of human prosperity.

A free society is tolerant and equal. It allows people to assemble with others as they choose, to move around feely, and to express any opinion, even if they say things that others find obnoxious. It restricts only language that might cause, or threaten, physical harm to others. It is blind about the application of laws: people are treated equally; even those in authority obey the same laws as everyone else.

The free society sees civil society — the voluntary association of people in clubs, associations, churches, charities and many other institutions — as the backbone of society, not the state. It accepts a role for the state in protecting our rights and in preventing injustice, and recognises that this is no small function. But it is very sceptical of expanding the state's role beyond that.

The economic principles

The economic principles of a free society are equally robust. The economy of a free society is a moral economy, based on voluntary interaction and exchange. It therefore engenders other moral virtues like collaboration, tolerance and trust. (This is no mere theory: economic experiments suggest people are much more trusting of one another in countries where market principles are more deeply established). The controlled economy, by contrast, can only work at all by deploying the evils of authority, command, force, fear and conformity.

The free economy is dynamic and resilient. With lots of different participants, ideas, approaches and methods, it advances on evolutionary principles, finding the best of many ways to absorb and process whatever changing needs, tastes, resources and events arise. The controlled economy, however, is based on a single idea of how to manage events. Everyone is stuck with that solution, good or ill. And when events change, the controlled economy cannot absorb them.

The role of government in a free economy is limited. It exists to crystallise and enforce the broad rules of voluntary exchange, not the detail. It lays out the rules that facilitate the ownership and transfer of property, and protects people against fraud, theft and violence. It provides a way to make collective decisions on a small number of economic choices (such as defence, policing, justice, and perhaps some infrastructure provision) that cannot be made by individuals. But it will have strong constitutional restraints on taxing and spending, for it knows that there is no limit to the calls for more spending of other people's money. It will, also, safeguard competition and be suspicious of calls for regulation. And it will ensure that the monetary system is soundly based and trustworthy, since money and trust underpin every economic transaction.

Reforming UK governance

Westminster's brand is polluted. The expenses scandals are not forgotten, and the public respect politicians less than even journalists and estate agents. They see politicians as a separate, detached class, focused on their own world: posturing and preening, rather than addressing the deep and everyday concerns of ordinary people. And there are many other reasons why people are deserting the mainstream parties and voting in ways that humiliate them.

Parliament too has become dysfunctional. It originated to protect us from the unrestrained power of the executive. Now it has become the executive. Those who are, or want to be, ministers and government officials outnumber by two to one those who see their role as representatives, protecting the public from government power.

The best solution might be to make Parliament an exclusively *representative* body, existing, as it once did, to put forward constituents' interests and to protect the public from the excesses and abuses of the executive. Ministers would have to be appointed in some other way; they would not be MPs, but would remain wholly accountable to Parliament. This, however, would be a major constitutional change for the UK. As a practical matter, therefore, it might be more effective to look at different reforms that would achieve the same ambitions.

We should start by paying MPs an appropriate amount for the job, abolishing their perks and making expenses completely transparent.

Rather than pay MPs' rent or mortgage costs, for example, we should provide simple accommodation near Westminster for the use of those who want it. Paying mortgage costs allows MPs to benefit from property appreciation – giving them an incentive to keep in place the onerous planning regulations that restrict housing supply and push up prices. That is not a streetwise system.

Parliamentarians must also be bound by the same laws as everyone else. Back in 2010, three Labour MPs attempted to escape prosecution for false expenses claims by invoking the 1689 Bill of Rights – the privilege ('private law') that also prevents MPs being sued for defamation. But the privilege was designed to prevent the executive harassing MPs – not to allow them to escape criminal justice or to ruin people's reputations without any comeback. (MPs can hardly claim that the latter is an infringement of their free speech, given the curbs on free speech they load on the general public. Better to have universal free speech – but one in which people accept the consequences of what they say.)

The UK has 650 MPs and about 800 Lords for a population of 66 million. The US manages perfectly well with 535 Members of Congress and 100 Senators, for a population of 326 million. By American standards, we should cut Parliament down to just 108 MPs and 20 Lords. The millions of disaffected voters are unlikely to shed a tear over that. The ministerial payroll needs to be culled too. One reason why boards, committees, juries and football teams are usually 11-12 strong is because that is the maximum number of others that people can efficiently deal with. Go up to thirteen, and you are out of luck. With a Cabinet of 22, it is no wonder that UK governance is so bad.

As for the House of Lords, despite its overblown size it works surprisingly well. There are certainly too many superannuated politicians appointed to it, but it does have a greater spread of talent than the Commons. It would be a mistake to destroy this by making the Lords elected just like the Commons. And that would simply make the Lords another Commons – to what end? Certainly we need a two-chamber system in order to restrain a powerful House of Commons. That requires a radically different election/selection system for it, or some hybrid system of elected and merit members. If terms were limited to say seven years, that would promote Peers' independence. And who really minds if they carried on calling themselves 'Lord' or 'Lady' afterwards?

Reforming the electoral system

A suite of electoral reforms is needed to make politicians, once again, representatives of the general public rather than members of a separate class. Term limits, by which MPs would be limited to a 10- or 15-year tenure, is an obvious one. It makes politics into a period of public service, not a lifetime career. It would mean that MPs would probably have had some experience in real, non-political work before they were elected, and that they would not abandon the wider world (and its citizens) that they knew they would return to. True, we would lose the experience of long-serving MPs; but the deep damage done by the current tenure system is infinitely greater.

As Daniel Hannan and Douglas Carswell outlined in their book *The Plan*, we also need to reduce the power of political parties over the electoral system. At the moment, candidates are chosen by the local party offices. At least, that is the theory: in reality, the central party managers have massive control over who becomes a candidate in what seat. Hannan and Carswell propose US-style open primaries, by which candidates are chosen by local party voters. They also (rightly) support recall petitions, whereby the public could sack MPs that lost their legitimacy and public support between between elections. (Such as those who shamelessly vote against their constituents' firm views or who try to flout the law with impunity.) And they propose popular legislative initiatives, whereby members of the public can propose measures to be voted on by the local population, and block contentious new laws.

Party dominance is also entrenched by the taxpayer money that parties receive — their annual Short Money (payments to opposition parties in the Commons), Cranborne Money (the equivalent in the Lords), aid to political parties in Scotland and Northern Ireland and Policy Development Grants provided through the Electoral Reform Society. Only the larger established parties qualify, so this funding makes it harder for other parties, with new ideas, to break through. The solution to that is obvious.

Reforming the administrative structure

A large part of the work of government is done by regulatory agencies and other quangos. Some have wide powers: often they can fine people or put firms out of business. Once established, however, the existence of these bodies is rarely questioned, and their tendency is to grow, by creating more work for themselves and those they regulate. In the first place, we should repeal the laws that allow burdensome regulations to be introduced by the order of a minister rather than by a vote in Parliament. In addition to reining in regulation and making sure it was properly considered, this would also help trim the power of the executive. Second, we should place sunset laws on all such bodies. In other words, they should have an agreed lifetime of (say) five years (the length of a Parliament) and after that MPs would have to vote on whether to continue them. This would create much more focus on what functions were really needed, and on the accountability of these powerful bodies. Third, regulation is much more burdensome on smaller businesses, absorbing a much larger proportion of their budgets. We should exempt micro-businesses (and possibly all small enterprises) from most regulation, particularly non-safety rules like those on wages and employment. That would limit the power of business lobby groups to change regulations so as to squeeze out competition. Fourth, we should check the growth of new regulation, and facilitate the removal of the most onerous rules, by requiring a full competition impact statement for each one.

The UK civil service prides itself on its professionalism, but its efficiency levels are notoriously low. In 2016, sick days averaged 2.9% in the public sector, compared to just 1.7% in the private sector. Since 2013, the number of days lost through labour disputes was 15 days per thousand in the public sector, but less than 1 in the private sector. Public employees work an average of 35 hours per week; in the private sector, people work 37.5 hours. Public-sector training is poor, jobs are rarely shed, and rather than asking whether a job is strictly necessary, employees who leave are automatically replaced.

And of course there are the generous salaries and pensions to consider: at least 130 local authorities pay 10 or more staff over £100,000; some are close to £1m, including pension contributions. At least 238 quangocrats featured among the top one per cent of earners in 2017, with some earning up to £750,000. Median gross salary in 2016 was £25,000 in the public sector, 11% higher than the private sector's £22,500. It is time to tackle these imbalances.

Because the government machine has grown and sprawled without any real conscious control, a new approach is needed. We should institute zero-based budgeting, whereby departments and agencies have to justify their whole existence each year. That means defining what they do, the limits of their scope, the value they create and the cost of achieving it. Back in the 1990s, Canada did something like this for the whole government. It resulted in large cutbacks in some areas (such as agriculture subsidies) but greater spending in others (such as pensions); and although it was far from perfect, the exercise did force people to think about the costs and benefits of government activity.

We also need departments and agencies to answer, annually, the following questions. Are their functions all really necessary? (Perhaps, changing events and technology has made them redundant.) If they *are* necessary, can someone other than government do them better? (For example, can we achieve lower cost and better quality by contracting out, privatising all or part of the activity, or opening things up to competition?). If government *must* do things, can it do them better? (Such as by looking at how other countries achieve better efficiency and results.)

Online spending transparency, with national and local government posting every payment they make, would certainly help this process: it would encourage public debate and prompt private and non-profit groups to point out where they can make improvements. Also, taxpayers should get an annual receipt, showing where their cash has been spent: right now, few people have any idea, and this again would encourage better scrutiny. And state assets should be listed in detail online, again to encourage debate on whether they are still needed or should simply be sold.

Local government reform

Around four-fifths of what local authorities do is dictated by and funded (or, some would say, underfunded) by the central government authorities. Very little is left to councils' own discretion. This further consolidates the power of the Westminster and Whitehall executive and stifles local diversity and innovation. It is time to scrap the Department for Communities and devolve its powers, with the others, to local authorities themselves.

Councils would, of course, need their own source of funding to replace central government grants; and the simplest might be to replace VAT with a local sales tax, much as in the US, to make them self-financing. Merging district councils, as well as regional assemblies and development agencies, into county councils would both add to accountability (few electors know which body is responsible for which functions) and help smooth out differences in wealth between the new tax-raising authorities. Business rates, meanwhile, should be determined on the basis of imputed land values, or as a tax on profits, which would be much fairer (especially to small and growing businesses) than the present rather arbitrary system that councils can exploit.

Constitutional reform

Even in the absence of separation of powers, further constitutional reforms are needed. Most elections and other votes in the UK are taken by a simple majority, but that should not mean that 50%+1 of the population are allowed to exploit the rest. Where exploitation is easy—as with taxation, for example, which the majority can easily impose on the minority—there should be a higher barrier. For example, new taxes or significant rises in the tax burden should require a two-thirds majority in both Commons and Lords. Or perhaps new taxes should be subject to a binding referendum.

The European Convention on Human Rights is an unsatisfactory guardian of our liberties. It confuses 'negative' rights (which require only that others do not infringe them) with 'positive' rights (such as the supposed 'right' to free education—not really a right, because it depends on others being forced to pay the cost). Partly because of such confusions, it has been interpreted in ways that are contrary to UK justice. It should be replaced with a new UK Bill of Rights, focusing on protections of individual rights and freedoms, such as fair electoral systems, freedom of speech and religion, due process and equal treatment under law, property rights, and personal integrity. This should specify the implied obligations (taxes, jury duty etc). But it should not confuse political ambitions (for, say, universal healthcare, education and welfare) with *rights*.

Spending and borrowing reform

In the Gordon Brown years, public sector growth was fuelled largely by stealth taxes, borrowing and the private finance initiative. The latter had been designed (indeed, colleagues and I helped design it) to bring private-sector expertise into the planning, finance, management and operation of large-scale infrastructure projects such as roads, prisons and hospitals. Although the government could borrow more cheaply, the private sector completes projects quicker and more efficiently, producing net savings; so using private finance and project management, the government saved money and did not have to raise large cash sums before it could embark on new projects. Gordon Brown, however, worked out that PFI could simply be turned into a mortgage scheme. It was stealth borrowing: he would commission new schools, hospitals and roads now and let future generations pay for them. Jeremy Corbyn and his colleagues plan to do even more of the same. (The political mafia are cunning: not even Al Capone thought of stealing from the unborn.)

The streetwise economist knows that the public sector is a very bad negotiator and purchaser of anything. (One hospital that was briefly privatised a while back managed to save £3m on supplies by doing things itself rather than using the NHS's much vaunted 'block purchasing power'. And the NHS spent £10bn on a failed IT system — a sum that could have bought a web-enabled laptop for every one of the 1.5 million people who work in it.) So as well as becoming merely stealth borrowing, PFI projects became far more costly than they should have been. Those future generations are getting an even worse deal. PFI can bring benefits: but it needs strong rules to prevent it being abused. And the public sector needs private negotiators to set up the deals on its behalf.

Gordon Brown introduced a very sensible rules on public borrowing—that it should be done solely for investment, not current spending, that it should be kept to a reasonable proportion of GDP, and that the government's budget should be balanced over the economic cycle. However, he abandoned the rules as soon as he ran out of money. The designation of where the 'economic cycle' started and ended was changed at Brown's convenience, and his definition of 'investment' was incredibly loose: he talked of 'investing' in healthcare, education and social services, when he really meant 'spending' on these things. Public sector 'investment' *should* refer to laying down capital that makes future services better and cheaper. The Office for Budget Responsibility (OBR) must revive, and police, the rules to ensure that governments cannot borrow to spend, so that borrowing stays at manageable levels, and so that the budget really does remain balanced.

The OBR could also have a role in curbing stealth debt. As already explained, the government's real obligations, including things like future pensions, healthcare, education and welfare promises, the cost of future nuclear power station decommissioning and suchlike, are many times the published debt figure. Exposing that will create a more sober attitude in debt management. Also, the future financial cost of all legislation (measures to expand the state provision of social care, for example, or public sector pay rises) should be spelled out when the legislation is in Parliament—and reviewed at regular intervals after.

We need overall limits on public spending too. The Rahn Curve, named after the economist Richard Rahn, suggests that while a little public spending on basic infrastructure, justice and so on helps economic growth, public spending of more than 15% of GDP starts to slow things, until eventually growth turns negative. Roughly, a ten point rise in public spending means a one point fall in growth. Sadly, that is where we already are. Lower growth of course means less wealth is generated that can be used on both private and public spending. So a long-term public spending limit of (say) 25% of GDP seems optimal – though it is much lower than today's 40% level. Hard choices will be needed.

Monetary soundness

Spending restraint would reduce governments resorting to another stealth tax, namely inflation. The Bank of England has done a poor job of controlling inflation because its 2% Consumer Price Index target is too crude, particularly when we are going through boom or bust periods as we have recently. A better target would be to produce steady growth in the nation's spending capacity (what economists call 'Nominal GDP (NGDP) targeting'). And the Bank should let the markets rein in any commercial banks that take excessive risks that are not unjustified by that steady growth projection.

The banks need more competition to regulate them. Right now, instead of the present complex regulatory rule book, we should simply raise the banks' capital requirements so that they have enough assets to ride out economic storms. In the longer terms, however, we should move towards 'free banking' – allowing in new competitors, letting banks decide their own capital reserve levels, but letting insolvent banks fail, with no taxpayer bail-outs. That may seem dangerous for depositors, but the fact that a bank can fail if it overextends itself forces banks to operate soundly. And if we allowed banks to issue their own currency, rather than forcing everyone to accept the Bank of England's monopoly money, it would soon become clear that people prefer a currency that keeps its value (which the Bank of England's does not).

Tax reform and simplification

The streetwise economist knows that in future we need lower, simpler, flatter taxes. High tax rates encourage (legal) avoidance and (illegal) evasion, which are bad both morally and financially. The UK tax code is one of the longest in the world, and getting longer. Even *Tolley's Tax Guides*, the accountants' crib books, come in at 1,897 for corporation tax, 1,801 pages for income tax, 1,463 pages for capital gains tax, and 953 pages for inheritance tax — between 50% and 185% longer than they were just 18 years ago. Meanwhile the number of taxpayers paying the 40p rate has risen from 1.7 million to 4.3 million, while the top one per cent of earners pay 28% of the total income tax take. No wonder we are leaching talent, and money, abroad. That exodus would simply increase under the McDonnell-Corbyn tax policies.

We should have a flat-rate income tax, with none of today's complicated concessions and exemptions, making it clear what everyone is due to pay. We have already taken the poorest out of income tax: we should take them out of national insurance too, and merge those two taxes together so that, again, it is clear what we are paying. For that matter, if we have VAT or a new sales tax on purchases — and any other taxes on things like pensions, insurance or airline travel — those should be clearly itemised, not stealthily concealed as now.

Company taxes are not paid by companies, but by people. And sadly, most of the burden falls on customers and workers, not (as intended) on bosses. We should scrap them and make ourselves an ultra-competitive country — and scrap the taxes on capital, transactions, shares and housing sales while we are at it. All these taxes create distortions, and damage UK performance.

Balancing the books

It is not difficult to grasp the importance of spending within your means, keeping the books balanced, not borrowing to fund current spending, and doing things that will boost your long-term prospects rather than undermine them. Every family knows that; and as Adam Smith said: "What is prudence in the conduct of every private family, can scarce be folly in that of a great kingdom."

But then Adam Smith was a very streetwise economist.

11 Making public policy rational

Without adhering to such basic economic and political principles, we will never clean up our seedy neighbourhood. Only the powerful (and the streetwise) will continue to prosper—at the expense of everyone else. We should instead be committed to an open society that respects the importance of individuals and does not regard them as cogs in someone else's machine. We need to be tolerant of the differences between people, not stamp out those differences in the name of some ideological vision of politics and society. In fact we need to celebrate those differences, because it is from trade and collaboration between diverse people that we prosper and advance.

We need also to understand that voluntary—not forced— collaboration between free people is an amazingly fertile source of ideas, innovation and creativity. We need free speech, for example, because the competition between ideas makes them stronger and better able to help us achieve our ambitions: ambitions such as a more peaceful and open society, and greater efficiency in our production. We must accept that government can never equal the creative genius of a free people. And recognising that power is all to easily abused, we must accept that government must be limited to the few things that only it can do.

The importance of justice

The most important of those few purposes of government—and it is no small task—is the establishment of justice. It is a task on which our managerialist rulers do very badly, partly because they do not understand the principles of justice. Indeed, they see those principles as getting in the way of what seems to them expedient at the time.

Thus, the threat of terrorism is taken to justify arbitrary stop and search, holding citizens without trial for two weeks (and foreigners longer), indefinite house arrest (without even charge, never mind conviction), banning non-violent political groups, spying on our e-mails, hacking our data, requiring phone and internet providers to yield information on us (without a warrant), taking DNA of anyone leaving or entering the UK (regardless of suspicion), allowing ministers to suspend most legislation, and much more. So broad are these powers that the Chancellor, Alistair Darling, used anti-terrorism legislation to freeze Icelandic bank assets in London during the 2008 financial crisis; before then it was used to arrest a woman walking on a cycle path, to bar a heckler from the Labour Party conference, and to shut down a quiet two-person anti-war demonstration near Downing Street.

Even threats of violence from political or religious ideologues — objecting to what they see as 'fascism' or 'blasphemy' in others — have led to major curbs on free speech. (And made stupidity a crime, as in the case of Mark Meechan, fined £800 for posting a YouTube video of his dog giving a Nazi salute).

As the pro-freedom organisation Liberty says, in confronting hostile ideologies, our political leaders should actively and robustly promote principles such as the rule of law and equal treatment, and values such as respect for individual rights. But they do not: instead, they allow those ideologues to make us change our laws in ways that breach our tolerant values and principles.

These are by no means the only ways in which our rights, values and principles are suspended to help the managerialists enjoy a quiet and easy time. As with the other things done in the name of keeping us safe — CCTV, online surveillance, an armed police — such measures merely give them more power over us. We have become so used to our basic liberties being curbed that only a streetwise few see how precarious our freedom has become.

The administration of justice

When authorities are armed with the huge powers that our police have, they can bully and intimidate us at will. In the US, for example, people accused of fraud and accountancy offences are routinely charged under anti-racketeering 'RICO' legislation (which carries a 20-year jail term on each count) to make them plea-bargain for a lesser sentence (whether guilty or not). The same intimidation tactics are not lost on our own police and prosecutors. They raise the authorities' conviction rates, but hardly constitute justice. Our laws should be subject to the principles of justice, not the other way round.

Also, the court system is notoriously slow and expensive—so much so that ordinary people cannot afford access to justice, and the authorities, with the deep pockets of the state, have the real and implicit power to threaten them with long and costly court proceedings. No wonder so many people simply settle their parking fines, speeding tickets, littering spot-fines, tax demands, and much else, even if they think them unjust. Local magistrates usually side with the police, so unless you are willing to invest a lot of time and money in the upper courts, settling straight away is the rational thing to do.

You only have to look at courts, with their outdated dress code and long-winded, intimidating procedures, so see how self-serving they have become. That is because they are a state monopoly, and the lawyers who practise in them are a state-supported monopoly, which uses statutory power to keep their numbers in expensive scarcity. As with other professional licensing, the result is a worse and much more costly service for the public. It is time that we experimented in competitive delivery of court functions, and opened up the restrictive practises of the legal profession. As court costs have risen, private arbitration has become more common in civil disputes; it is time now to give the decisions of arbitrators the status of a lower court judgement, so that the parties can move directly to appeal in the higher courts, rather than starting all over again.

Judges, prosecutors and police chiefs are all appointed by the managerialist machine, so it is no surprise if they predominantly serve the interests of the government rather than the public. Daniel Hannan and Douglas Carswell argue that we need locally elected Sheriffs to take control of the police, in order to fill that democratic gap and make sure that the police are properly accountable to local people. Sheriffs would prioritise local offences and the police response, prosecute offences and set local sentencing guidelines. There is a case for opening up the selection of judges as well: that if they are not chosen by a popular vote, the process by which they are chosen should be much more transparent.

Drugs and tobacco

Of course, the courts would be a lot less busy were it not for the number of drug-use cases and the violence associated with the drug trade. We have around 12,000 people in jail for drug offences: an estimated 4,000 teenagers are involved in drug smuggling in London alone. Yet we simply hand this £5.3 billion trade over to criminals: and because the penalties are high, they are necessarily the most daring and ruthless of criminals. There is a very simple remedy, which is to decriminalise all or most drugs. As Milton Friedman once observed, most of the harm that drugs do is because they are illegal. Not since Prohibition have we seen street gangs carving up each other over the beer trade. Nor do beer drinkers burgle houses to get cash for their next fix of Theakston's Old Peculier. Many 'party' drugs are no more toxic than alcohol, and often less: the reason why some young people die taking them is because they are often of unknown or inconsistent strength and are adulterated with poisons. That is not a problem with legal substances like beer.

True, alcohol is addictive and dangerous in excess. The sixty-odd medical conditions associated with it cause up to 10% of UK deaths and diseases. But the regulations on alcohol hinder research on better alternatives — such as 'Alcosynth', which is a hundred times safer and hangover-free. We need less regulation and more 'sinnovation' — research into less damaging alternatives on alcohol, tobacco, even fat and sugar. But again our highly specified regulations trap us in the old, dangerous methods and technologies.

Some drugs such as cannabis are so readily accessible that there seems little point in having a law against them; and any enforcement of the law (we have over 1,300 cannabis offenders in prison, costing taxpayers £50 million a year) is inevitably limited and arbitrary. Decriminalising cannabis, as has happened in other countries, would create a licit £6.8 billion market, with savings of up to £1 billion for taxpayers.

We need realistic solutions for hard drugs too. In the days when heroin was medicalised — your use of it was regarded as something for doctors, not the courts, to deal with — we had few registered addicts (just 1,000 in the early 1970s). Now official estimates suggest we have 250,000 opiate users, most of whom are taking heroin. Around 500-1,000 people die from opiates each year. The solution to our hard drugs problem seems obvious: bring them back into the open, where we can deal with users' problems, and with the wider economic and social consequences. Have dedicated centres where addicts can take their drugs, but under medical supervision.

Again, cigarettes are more dangerous than many drugs; but the managerialists' efforts have focused on raising taxes on them (which happily preserves the Treasury's revenue stream), banning advertising, disallowing small packs (which unfortunately disadvantages poorer people most), and requiring packs to carry specified, graphic health warnings. Bizarrely, that has the effect of forbidding manufacturers from informing smokers that vape and heat-not-burn alternatives would be twenty or more times safer for them — as is the case. A change in the warnings, or an advisory insert in cigarette packets, would save many lives. It is time we told the regulators that they are killing people through ignorance, and defied them by making those life-saving changes.

Welfare policy

The state may have no business telling us what we may or may not put into our bodies, but (along with the guarantee of justice) there is general agreement that it has a duty to make sure that those in need of welfare support get it. That does not necessarily mean that the state actually has to provide welfare itself: as Kristian Niemitz argues in *Welfare Without The State*, there are many other ways to do that, through the private institutions of civil society. But the state has already taken on this function — in a big way.

And incompetently too: despite being one of the world's richest countries, with a third (34%) of public expenditure going on pensions and welfare, we have still seen a huge rise in dependency, with ten million families living mainly on state benefits. As headline-seeking politicians have added one new benefit after another, the system has become a bureaucratic quagmire that seems to defy simplification.

However, there are easy solutions. Recognise that a paying job is the best form of welfare. Take the poorest out of taxation and national insurance so as to make work pay. Scrap minimum wages but use in-work tax credits to help the poorest stay in work (these could be made an automatic part of the PAYE system). Where state support is necessary, provide it in simple cash benefits through a negative income tax system—which is already being trialled in other countries. Target state benefits, including pensions, to help those who need help, rather than inefficiently paying money to those who do not. It is also worth exploring whether other providers can run state 'insurance' benefits better than the state. For example, private insurers say they could save billions in disability benefits, simply by ensuring that people get speedy treatment for things like back problems and mental illness, before they worsen.

The state pension, that unsustainable Ponzi scheme, would be best replaced by individual pension savings accounts, as Chile pioneered in the early 1990s and many other countries followed. We could extend these into something like the *Fortune Account* proposed by the Adam Smith Institute—a lifetime account that people can pay into and draw out of for their various personal needs.

Housing policy

Housing is becoming unaffordable, especially in London and the South East. Attempts to make it less costly (like Help to Buy) simply fuel demand further while not opening up new supply— which is throttled by planning regulation. The other managerialist solution—a Housing Ombudsman—laughably misses the point. We need to open up the supply of housing, and that means abolishing or reforming the green belt to allow construction on intensive farmland and damaged land, neither of which is a public amenity. A first step is to survey our ever-expanding green belt, to determine which parts of it are actually green, or a public amenity, or of scientific or historical importance.

We need also to get rid of the discretion that officials have over planning consents. They have it only because they run a restrictive system backed by state power. But it makes planning decisions arbitrary, and expensive or hard to challenge, and generates a kind of planning corruption. Most other European countries have rules-based systems; so should we.

Many of the local objections to planning developments arise because people in the neighbourhood suffer all the downsides (such as traffic around supermarkets and housing developments, pressure on schools and hospitals, and airport noise) without receiving any compensation. A better system would be to chart who was affected and have a rule that those (state or private) proposing the development had to offer cash compensation, directly to those affected (and not to the local council, which could spend the money elsewhere). Such a compensation rule would defuse a great many objections to new road and rail links, housing developments and much more.

In London, and other cities under population pressure, restrictions on building designs should be loosened to allow more popular and denser ways of building, such as the terraces of Islington or Edinburgh, and the popular low-rise apartment blocks so common on the Continent. Some areas of the green belt, such as those within a ten-minute walk of a rail station, could be opened to development, again in dense formation rather than in sprawling bungalows. And certain clusters, like that around the new US embassy in London, seem appropriate for higher building. It should also be much easier to obtain planning permission to increase the height of existing two- or three-storey buildings; that alone would create trillions of pounds' worth of new property, and living space, in our cities.

Stamp duty on property transactions is four times more harmful to the UK economy than income tax or VAT, costing taxpayers £12 billion a year. Economists in Australia found that its equivalent there cost 75¢ on every dollar it raised. It has human costs too: it gums up the housing market, stopping people from moving to the jobs they need, and trapping people in homes that are too large or too small for them. It should go.

Human services

Despite huge injections of cash into the NHS, it still struggles to stay within its budget. It spends about the European average (nearly a tenth of the nation's income), but has fewer doctors, nurses, beds or scanners, still uses 9,000 fax machines, and its performance is below average in terms of life expectancy and survival rates for eight of the twelve most mortal conditions. Its preventable mortality statistics are dire — in 2015, some 117 out of every 100,000 died unnecessarily, compared with just 78 in France. The managerialists hail it as the 'envy of the world', but nobody is rushing to copy it: some 40% of French hospital beds are in the private sector, and 45% of German hospitals are private or non-profit.

Europe generally has a mixed system: largely private provision with the state paying for basic treatment, for those who cannot afford to pay for themselves, and for uninsurable long-term conditions; but with people relying on private or group insurance for most other needs. France sends people a bill for their doctors' time, but reimburses those in need: we too would deflect a lot of unnecessary pressure on the NHS if we merely handed patients a statement of the cost of their treatment — even if it was marked 'Paid in full by UK taxpayers.'

We could easily get to a European-style system. A dedicated NHS tax, earmarked from income tax, would pay for those who cannot afford healthcare, and would show the real cost of a service that people think is 'free'. Those who insure privately could get a rebate from some of this tax, reflecting the burden they were taking off the state system. Provision itself should be opened up to competition, with competing providers taking state-funded patients along with private ones. Ultimately, we could aim for a Singapore-style savings account system, in which people devote part of their income to an account large enough to pay for any treatment that most people would need in the course of a year; and if people did not use it, they could roll it over for other purposes such as retirement income.

As for long-term care, both for adults of working age and the frail elderly, free state provision is not the answer: it merely induces families to dump elderly and disabled relatives onto the state system, while raising taxes and thereby stifling economic growth. Like healthcare, there is no limit to what could be spent. Again, partnership is a better solution. One in four people are likely to need residential care, but presently this is uninsurable because a few people need very long-term and expensive care. The government should agree to pay for the longest care home stays (say, beyond five years), which would make it possible to insure for any needs less than that—or indeed to save towards them. In terms of the provision of care homes, at present this is left to local authorities. But their budgets are strained: they have too few homes, and many of those are twenty or more years old and not up to present standards. Better to induce private investors to build, own and operate care homes on a large scale, with the local authorities simply paying for the places they need. Lastly, as already explained, the elderly population should make a greater contribution to their generation's health and care costs, instead of passing the burden onto the young and the unborn.

Education

It is questionable whether we need compulsory education at all: most parents are passionately about giving their children a good grounding, and all that compulsion has done is to trap them in a regimented state system. Few believe that this system really works. School exams are not trusted, schools are run haphazardly, there are too many quangos and civil servants involved. Like healthcare, the solution is probably a partnership, with independent providers who follow the demand from parents, and at least some state finance, to ensure that all families have access. There are countless examples of this already, in Sweden, in the Charter Schools of the US, and now in the UK with free schools.

But the government needs to ease off its central direction of how schools work, what is taught, and how. For example, we need profit-making schools — which have worked well in Sweden. There, profit and competition allow chains of schools to be developed, which is more efficient, because they can follow a common model and can pool their administrative, budget and human resource needs, rather than each school having to improvise is own. Parents of school age children should have a legal right to take them to non-state schools, carrying with them the money that the state would have spent on their education (with adjustment for special needs and other circumstances).

While taxpayers need some reassurance about what schools teach state-supported students, the national curriculum has grown far beyond its usefulness, and now simply prevents good teachers from doing what they know works. Local authorities too should be taken out of the loop—and forced to make way for new kinds of school, instead of over-specifying every element through the planning and curriculum systems.

Universities are supposed to be centres of free thought, but are subject to highly centralised controls (such as rules on the economic and ethnic diversity of their students) that are designed to signal the virtue of the managerialist politicians and officials in charge of them. More intangibly, they all feel obliged to submit to the political mob culture—curbing free speech, for example, in the name of preventing 'micro-aggressions' and establishing 'safe spaces' for 'victims'.

Ideally, universities with confidence in themselves and their product should break free of the state's macro- *and* micro-control and assert their independence, including their financial independence. Right now, none dare (except the University of Buckingham, which has always been independent), because although they resent Whitehall's interference, they depend on government research grants. We should simply let universities go independent in the confidence that their research budgets will not be affected.

Student finance is another mess. While it is right that students should pay for their own education—for it is they, not taxpayers, who derive by far the most benefit from it—the student loan system is rightly hated. Interest rates are high because so many graduates never earn enough to pay back their fees: the average student accrues £5,800 of interest on their loan, and the default rate is as high as 45%. As already mentioned, universities should charge the going rate for their courses, rather than fees being capped, so that students would have to make a realistic calculation about what course and what university would benefit them most. But rather than a bureaucratic and inefficient loan scheme, an Australian-style capped graduate tax would be better. Graduates would pay a higher rate of tax until they had paid off the cost of their tuition — or (perhaps even simpler) some standard amount that reflects the average cost. Then they would revert to normal tax rates. The streetwise solution is even more radical: allowing students to pay nothing up front but to sell 'equity' in their future salaries, creating a direct link between the student's future performance and what the lender receives, and reflecting the fact that investing in education is risky. Both solutions have the benefit of ending the psychological burden of 'debt'.

Migration

One thing that is sure to drive voters into the hands of nationalist parties and demagogues is immigration. Intellectually, those who believe in a free society should support free migration; but real events challenge this. Where migration comes slowly, it can be absorbed peacefully — as it has been through hundreds of years of British history. But when states build walls across continents that then suddenly collapse, or when governments foment wars that see millions of civilians fleeing for their lives, migration comes in mass movements; and that is where the tensions start.

Economically, the case for free migration is mixed. It raises the nation's growth per capita, though not by much. It does depress unskilled wages, and without it, employers would have to raise wages and improve the training of UK workers. Large-scale migration puts a strain on education, health services, roads and houses, but that is only because these industries are state-run or heavily state-regulated and cannot respond quickly to demand: as Mark Littlewood of the Institute of Economic Affairs, put it, "Whoever heard of Tesco or Sainsburys complaining about having too many customers?" Meanwhile, the argument that we need to import younger workers so that we can sustain our state pensions, healthcare and other services used mainly by the elderly, is no more than an extension of the current Ponzi scheme thinking. The Oxford demographer David Coleman calculates that the UK would need six million immigrants a year to sustain today's age structure.

But the managerialists' attempt to limit migration to the 'tens of thousands' was plainly mad in the light of EU rules that entitled 400 million EU citizens, many unskilled, to live and work in the UK. The 'tens of thousands' promise therefore saw us turning down thousands of skilled would-be migrants, with a 21,000 cap on non-EU skilled workers. In the first quarter of 2018 alone, we refused 6,000 visas for engineering, technical, IT and medical staff, even though all these are in short supply (with 10,000 vacant posts for medical staff, for example).

Talented people make a big difference to an economy (even a local economy – look at the huge growth of Silicon Valley or the booming pharmaceuticals, genome and medicine hubs around Cambridge). We need more, not less: the cap should go. A points-based system might be a reasonable alternative, provided that numbers were not closely limited. But those who qualify under a bureaucratic points scheme may not necessarily match what employers need. A better system is to use the market and auction visas to employers. Then, the industries with the greatest need, and which would reap the greatest potential benefit from skilled migrant workers, could simply pay to bring in those they need. That would boost productivity and growth, and would calm public concerns about mass migration from low-skilled workers – while the revenue raised would help to provide the required improvements in public services.

In terms of unskilled workers, there could be a separate auction for them. For seasonal workers, we could have a lottery-based system, modelled on New Zealand's Recognised Seasonal Employer scheme or Canada's Seasonal Agricultural Workers Program. And young people should be able to travel without hindrance, particularly within the European Economic Area and among the Anglophone countries such as Australia, New Zealand, Canada and the US – benefiting everyone through the cross-fertilisation of ideas.

Students, for their part, should be taken out of the migrant figures entirely. We want to sell our university to the rest of the world; we want foreign students to become our friends, because they will probably remain so for a lifetime; we want them to graduate then get experience in UK companies before they return home. But we make it hard for them to come, and kick them out as soon as we can, simply to achieve a managerialist target.

Promoting competition

When our largest industries were privatised, we tried to introduce at least some competition into them. (An exception was British Gas, whose chairman, Sir Denis Rooke, was determined to keep it intact; but even that has subsequently been opened to modest competition.) Regulatory offices were set up, charged with expanding competition further and acting in lieu of competition where none existed. The idea was that as competition expanded, regulation could be scaled back.

But competition has expanded little, and the regulatory offices have grown. As they have tried to track down and eliminate cross-subsidies and inefficiencies within large and complex industries, and the regulated industries have become more adroit at gaming the rules, the regulatory offices too have become even larger and more complex. Because they inevitably have to work so closely with the regulated industries, sharing information on pricing and other issues, some people wonder they have become captured and have lost their independence and clout. Others say they have become too focused on systems, not on the welfare of customers.

We need radical changes in gas, water, electricity, telephone and rail regulation. Regulators should suffer less interference from government. They should seek progress towards competition from the industries themselves, rather than attacking them with rules and price caps as they do now. Competition, again, is the best regulator. And the regulators should be given a clear mission: to make these industries fully competitive and then phase themselves out of a job.

Rail is a particularly contentious industry, mainly because its diverse problems are so obvious to so many people who travel on it. Privatisation led to a surge in passenger numbers and service growth, but as we have seen, the franchise system means that rail services are still dictated by the government. Virgin and a small number of others dominate, and the lack of competition has meant that, while the cost of living has rising by 86% since 1995, the prices of unregulated 'anytime' fares have risen by up to 250%. We are the only European country running such a system. We should learn from airline competition — where passengers have a choice of budget and premium operators to and from most destinations. If we scrapped the one-model-fits-all-situations franchising system and moved to 'pay per slot' or 'open access' systems, rail users could get similar choice on long distance routes, which would improve services and reduce costs for travellers. Competition in other privatised industries would do the same.

Choosing your targets

When governments intervene, run industries, or introduce controls and regulations, they really should work out what the results might be, and whether the overall effect could be positive or negative. Otherwise, negative results build up and then there are more calls for yet more, equally counterproductive action.

This should not be controversial; but it rarely happens because the incentives in our managerialist system are all about being *seen* to act rather than acting rationally. The mutual interest cartel between politicians and journalists strengthens that effect even further. It happens not just in the really important areas such as health, justice or policing, but even in the simplest and most trivial things.

Why, for example, do we require drivers of any vehicle older than three years to pay up to £80 a year for MOT safety inspections, when modern car technology, design, safety and diagnostics makes this increasingly pointless? Mechanical failure accounts for just 2% of all accidents in the UK, the same rate as places that do not require annual inspections (such as most of the US). Two-thirds of accidents are due to driver action (speeding, drunk driving, not using a seat belt), which MOT tests cannot prevent. So drivers pay a pointless £250 million a year (which poorer families in particular can ill afford); but if any politician suggested scrapping the test, 20,000 garages would be up in arms, the 2% figure would be forgotten and the newspapers would run headlines such as 'Government allows killer cars on our streets'.

One can see how populism is fed. Any national event, like a royal wedding, and politicians are proposing a new bank holiday. Jeremy Corbyn has called for the four saints' days all to be bank holidays. That would add another three holidays to the four that we already have in Spring; and remember that bank holidays already cost the economy about £2.5 billion each, around £19 billion a year. Sure, the travel and hospitality industries benefit from them, but that means longer hours for the workers in those sectors, who tend to be less well paid. And many people do not recognise the traditional Christian festivals anyway. So why should we all be forced into the same traffic jams on the same days, rather than choosing our own holidays? The answer is simple: there is no political mileage in setting us free.

That is the sad but very general message that the streetwise economist is well aware of. It is why the only way out of our managerialist miasma is to start from the principles of individual rights and economic and social freedom, and to be robust in our rejection of the opposite.

12 Ending the need to be streetwise

Strengths and weaknesses

Our political and economic neighbourhood is a rough place, full of crime, fraud, embezzlement, extortion, violence and intimidation — all of which is forced on us and presented to us as legitimate public policy. Some, like Westminster's growing band of socialist ideologues, confident that this sort of mafia control over people's lives is actually virtuous, would like to make it even rougher.

Do we simply have to cower and stay safe, stay streetwise? Are the gangs just too strong for us to overcome? Not at all. Economic freedom has powerful strengths. The more it has spread, the more it has brought prosperity to us and to the world — particularly to the very poorest and least advantaged. It sets minds free to be creative in solving our human problems. It allows diverse individuals to pursue diverse personal utopias, rather than trapping them in someone else's idea of utopia. And it is consistent with human nature: however much the ideologues try to control it, the free economy still breaks through.

Certainly, there are weaknesses. The *unseen* workings of a free economy are hard to explain and understand, so there is always a tendency to focus on simple but mistaken *seen* solutions. The real-life version of capitalism is heavily loaded with statism and cronyism. Businesspeople are hypocritical, claiming to support competition in general but seeking protections and privileges for themselves. But that is possible only because the state has grown so large, and has so much money and so many favours to give out. We should start the reform process from there.

Threats and opportunities

The global spread of economic freedom, and the prosperity and equality that it brings, is surely an opportunity — an opportunity to demonstrate the practical effects of liberalising policy. We already saw, between 1918 and 1989, the practical effects of the opposite. But today's growing empowerment of the poor, and of those not born into ruling races or classes, must also be an opportunity to extol social and economic freedom. And while the socialist model might work on a very small scale, the evolving, spontaneous order of the market economy is the only functioning system that can and does embrace the whole world.

The threats remain. Managerialist politicians and officials have every interest in preserving the status quo. Rent-seeking lobbyists have a similar interest. Intellectuals believe that they know better than the public how to run people's lives. Free speech is being curbed by those who confuse violence with merely causing offence, and who cannot see the freedom-preserving importance of people being able to voice their ideas, however unpopular they are. Regulations and controls spread and increase, and prove very hard to resist.

As people have become fed up with this crony system, populism and nationalism have spread. But many of those who reject today's managerialism would simply replace it with their own, rather than setting people free. And yet, over the millennia, human freedom, including social and economic freedom, has proved remarkably durable and resilient. That is because a free society can respond and adapt to whatever our changing world throws at it; a society built on a fixed view of how the world should be, cannot. However rough our neighbourhood seems at the moment, it is still possible to imagine, and to create, a better world in which we trade and collaborate freely and voluntarily, stamp out violence either by the state or others, and replace forlorn managerialism with open markets and competition.

That would be a world in which you do not actually have to be streetwise merely to survive.